W9-BLJ-157

Executive on the Move:
Tackling Your New Management Job

ABOUT THE AUTHOR

JAMES MENZIES BLACK is a graduate of the University of South Carolina. He was at one time associated with Daystrom, Inc. (then called ATF, Inc.) and with the Associated Industries of Cleveland. At both companies he served as a member of the industrial relations staff. From 1953 to 1956 he was Personnel Division Manager of the American Management Association. He then joined the Pennsylvania Railroad, where he was Assistant Director of Personnel Administration. In 1961 he became Executive Vice President of the American Association of Industrial Management/National Metal Trades Association.

Mr. Black is author of *How to Grow in Management, Assignment: Management,* and *Developing Competent Subordinates.* He is co-author with J. George Piccoli of *Successful Labor Relations for Small Business* and co-author with Guy B. Ford of *Front-line Management.* He has written many articles on personnel subjects for business magazines, and his humorous pieces have appeared in such magazines as *The Saturday Evening Post, Esquire,* and the *Ladies' Home Journal.*

Mr. Black is a former member of the Planning Council of the Silver Bay Conference and the Personnel Planning Council of the National Industrial Conference Board. He is a member of the American Management Association.

EXECUTIVE ON THE MOVE:

Tackling Your New Management Job

By James Menzies Black

American Management Association
New York

CONTENTS

agement Team—The Leader Sets the Pace—What to
Do About Staff Deadwood—How to Spot Minus Factors in Subordinates—How to Spot Plus Factors in Subordinates—Follow-up, Communication, and Performance—Keep the Support of Superiors—Your Relationship with Consultants—Some Tips on Taking the Initial
Steps

INTRODUCTION

No MATTER WHO YOU ARE, IF YOU HOLD A MIDDLE MAN-
agement position and are 45 years old or under, the
chances are better than even that you will be on a different
assignment, perhaps even living in a different community,
within the next five years. Your change of job may take
place in the framework of your present company by either
promotion or transfer—or both. It may be that you will
be offered a position with another employer that gives you
greater opportunity. Or there is always the unhappy
chance that because of cutbacks, mergers, or a change in
management you will suddenly find yourself forced to
seek employment somewhere else. Whatever the reason
for your coming job change, this book is intended to help
you make your move and get set in your new job more
easily and smoothly.

There are, as a matter of fact, very many of you.
Executives are constantly shuttling around the country.
Industry is expanding. Mergers are a commonplace. Large
companies are buying small local firms and building new
plants. Some employers now operate units in every state
in the union and many foreign countries. And they don't
hesitate to transfer a man from one location to another—
sometimes on short notice.

Also, the managerial casualty list is high. A merger may
lead to the displacement of many capable people who
must seek positions elsewhere. The need to be competitive

forces the alert company to be ruthless—it can't afford deadwood. The man who holds a responsible job must measure up to its demands or find himself sidetracked to a less demanding position or abruptly landed in the employment market—which is never a happy place to be unless you can be there on your own terms.

Half a Million Job Changes

All this means that management today is hard put to find qualified men to keep its organization successful and competitive. Recruiting has become big business. Nowadays fewer than one out of a hundred management men are working for the same company with which they started.

We asked William Megary of Philadelphia, one of this country's leading experts in executive recruitment, "How many executives do you think take jobs with new companies during a given year?" Said Mr. Megary, "If you're talking about middle management people and top executives, a conservative estimate would be 35,000. I have seen figures as high as 50,000. During years when the economy is expanding, I think the last figure probably is reasonably accurate."

"One more question," we said. "How many executives—either by being transferred or by taking a job with a different employer—do you think move from one community to another during a year?" Mr. Megary laughed. "I don't know that I have ever seen any such figure," he replied, "but I should imagine that if you said half a million, you wouldn't be far wrong."

Richard Enion, also of Philadelphia, agreed with Mr. Megary. Himself an expert in executive recruitment, Mr. Enion remarked, "From the information that is available to us, I would say that at least 60,000 executives change their jobs and companies every year. This figure may even be higher when business is booming and the demand for capable people increases. If you were to multiply 60,000 by 5, you would get the approximate number of executives who are annually transferred to other jobs within the framework of their own companies. In other words, the ratio of job changes to job transfers is about 1 to 5."

Trademark of the Times

The transiency of the contemporary executive population has caused changes in the psychology and attitudes of management people. Today the young trainee who begins his career with a company does not necessarily expect to climb to the top of this firm. He may think, "I'll get experience and then be in a position to get a better job somewhere else."

"We don't mind this attitude," the vice president of a textile mill commented. "There aren't enough top jobs at our company to satisfy all of the capable young men we hire. We tell them at the start that we don't expect many of them to stay with us permanently. But we add that the experience they get with us will increase their value and help them find better positions somewhere else."

Before writing this book we interviewed executives from many companies on the problem of corporate staffing. One observation that we heard repeatedly may be summed up like this: "The restlessness of the executive and professional groups in management is a trademark of our times. This may be explained by the feeling on the part of many extremely capable executives that they are 'swords for hire.' They do fine jobs for their employers, but do not hesitate to leave for a better opportunity when they believe they have accomplished their tasks. When they leave, they may very well take some of their key men with them."

Many of the industry people we talked to said that the

real brain-teaser of modern management is the changing patterns of loyalty among the executive group in our society. "Good men are no longer willing to stay put and wait for a promotion," they said. "They're loyal and dedicated. They work long hours, and they produce. But loyalty to the man has been substituted for company loyalty. If the top man goes, like a football coach he'll take his team with him."

This is particularly true of large corporations whose very size makes them somewhat impersonal. When a company is small or family-owned, executive stability is usually much greater, although occasionally management tolerates a lower standard of performance from long-service executives. This is understandable. A company of this kind retains the personal touch.

In any case, managements do not seem unduly concerned with the problem of what can be done to stabilize the executive team. Probably this executive mobility is a good thing. New people bring new ideas, and there's less likelihood of comfortable "rut" thinking.

Those Greener Pastures

The contemporary American executive, in short, is restless, and if he is a good one, he can afford to be restless. The demand for management talent is tremendous. A capable executive will have many opportunities to change to a job at another company if he thinks such a change will be helpful to his career.

"As soon as a man sticks his head above the crowd and word gets around that he's doing a top job for his company," said an executive vice president, "he won't have to worry about seeking a new position. Headhunters will be on his tail, literally begging him to consider positions their clients have to offer."

Remember, however, that it is much more difficult to

find a job when you are looking for it from the street than when you are thoroughly entrenched in a top spot with a good company and are reasonably contented with things as they are. In this situation, jobs come looking for you.

Here are some suggestions that may be helpful in weighing the advantages of a job offer somewhere else.

1. *Don't take a job with another company just to escape from problems that harass you on your present job.* The difficulties at the new company are probably just as great as the ones you left behind. If you know deep down that you aren't doing a good job where you are, and think that by going somewhere else you will get out in time to beat the descending ax, you may be right—it's the only thing to do. But unless you face up to problems and lick them, you probably won't last too long on your new job either.

2. *Don't make a career of job-hopping.* Some executives have their résumés in the mail constantly and are always quietly asking consultants to consider them for various positions which they hear are open. If you get this kind of reputation, it hurts. For one thing, if the news gets back to your boss (and it probably will if you look often enough), he won't like it.

3. *Don't let yourself be oversold.* Every top management job has problems. Never think you are moving to Utopia when you say goodbye to your old firm. Don't take literally everything the executive recruiter says about the opportunity he hopes you will accept. He thinks you are good, or he wouldn't be talking to you, but it's in his interest to make the job he offers sound good. So do your own investigating.

4. *Don't be afraid of problems.* If you take a hard job and lick it, you add to your own reputation

and your success will probably win you further opportunities. If you pull a near-bankrupt firm into the black, you gain a bigger reputation than if you help a going company keep going.

5. *Make sure you have the powers you need.* If you decide to take a new job, be as sure as possible that you will have all the authority you require to do it. If this power stems from a superior, do your best to find out if he has the authority to deliver on his commitments to you.

6. *Don't be fooled by superficialities.* A high-sounding title and more money are nice, but they are empty honors if the job doesn't measure up to your anticipations. There's nothing that gives a man a greater feeling of insecurity than holding a big title and earning a high salary—and not being allowed to do anything. Frequently, and particularly on staff jobs, this happens when a consulting firm has helped a company reorganize and has recommended that a number of new positions be created. The management has gone along with the recommendations on paper, but it may not really be ready to change its ways.

7. *Don't take a job in a panic.* You hear rumors that your company will be sold or merged, or that there will be severe cutbacks, and heads will roll. All these things may be true, and it may be wise for you to look around. But don't be premature. Fear has led many men to grab for a job elsewhere when their golden opportunity was still right at home.

8. *Don't bargain about your old job.* If you have a better opportunity at another company, take advantage of it. Don't be an opportunist and try to play your offer against your old job in an attempt to get more money or promotion. If your company has any sense, this won't work. If you think it wise

to discuss the situation with your boss before leaving, do so, but don't ask him to make long-term commitments or reassure you with bright promises about the future. Nobody can foresee tomorrow; the promises you extract from your boss may become completely impossible for him to fulfill.

9. *Understand the role of business leadership.* An executive must have a detailed knowledge of his own assignment plus a broad comprehension of the function of management. He is not an entrepreneur, a speculator, or a promoter, although these talents are helpful when controlled and properly applied. He takes reasonable risks but doesn't gamble foolishly. He is responsible for too many people's welfare to play fast and loose with either their future or that of his company. He gives dedicated service to the management that hires him and makes sure that no action of his reflects on its integrity. He never dodges hard decisions, nor does he take advantage of temporary expediency for short-term gains that will eventually be damaging to his employer.

10. *Take a hard look at your old job before leaving it.* Your reputation is solid; your boss respects your work. Maybe you can do better in the long run by staying where you are. At least give it serious thought. You owe it to the people who gave you the chance to get where you are.

An Opportunity—and a Risk

This book should be useful to any executive who changes jobs, for whatever reason, and must now adjust to changed conditions—a broader assignment, a new home in a different community, new associates, new friends. It will, of course, be of particular interest to the man who changes his company when he changes his job. However, practically every suggestion made holds true as well for the man who is transferred—and, usually, promoted—to a unit of his company located somewhere else.

Generally speaking, the very fact that you have the opportunity to try your hand at a new position in a new community is a compliment. You have convinced somebody—your management, if it's a transfer—that you know your business and that you're just the man it needs in an important job. The move involves risk, but risk is part and parcel of executive progress. Whether to take a position with another company or accept a transfer in your own is a matter of personal judgment. Friends can advise you, but only you can make the final decision.

CHAPTER I

HOW TO GET READY
TO START A NEW JOB

YOU HAVE TAKEN A NEW JOB! YOU HAVE SAID GOODBYE TO friends at your old company and promised to keep in touch. But you know—and so do they—that most of them will no longer be a part of your business life. Now you are in a state of pleasant suspension, the interim period between past and future. Although you may appear calm and confident to others, deep down you are excited and a little bit apprehensive.

In your last assignment you were successful, and that earned the coming opportunity. But you knew the problems of the old position, and understood your subordinates and associates—what their strong points and their weaknesses were, how much responsibility you could safely delegate, how to get the most out of their capabilities, how to anticipate and compensate for their shortcomings. The terrain of your business battlefield was as familiar as the pictures on the wall of your old office. Like any good general, you knew your troops and how to use them.

Now you are moving into the unknown and the unfamiliar. Certainly you have advance information on what to expect. Executives have talked to you at length about their problems, have explained how much they need your help to solve them. Your questions have been answered, and the scope of your authority and responsibility has been thoroughly described. But you won't discover the whole truth until you have moved in and taken charge. The people you talked to put the best face on things. You would do the same thing in their place. They think it is in their best interest to have you join their team. Although they quite honestly told you what they want you to accomplish and said what tools (money, manpower, equipment) you would be given to achieve these goals, they put more emphasis on the challenge of overcoming the obstacles than on the difficulty of the obstacles themselves.

Still, you were on top of your last job, and now you will have to start from scratch. Again you are putting your hard-earned reputation on the line. Furthermore, the below-surface attitude of many of your new associates initially will be, "Here's a hotshot from outside who has come to show us how. Okay, hotshot! Show us how!"

Being human, you have doubts. No wonder you say to yourself, "Did I make the right decision? Have I bitten off more than I can chew? Would I be better off had I stayed where I was?"

Alexander the Great exclaimed, "Only the gods can look down the road we might have taken!" So forget your fears. As soon as you get into the swing of your new work, your misgivings will vanish. The thing to do now is to get ready, mentally and physically, for nine o'clock Monday morning when you move into a new job, a new office, and an exciting, brand-new career.

Plan a Smooth Transition

Doctor Samuel Johnson wrote, "Change is not made without inconvenience, even from worse to better." When you took the new job, you pulled up the roots of at least part of your life. The old familiar environment is gone.

There will be some drastic changes in your work surroundings, your job habits, your personal living, and even your home if you move to a new location.

Don't let these problems dominate your thinking. The new job is of prime importance. Private affairs should not be allowed to interfere with getting started right. The new management will try to help you make the transition smoothly, but as a responsible adult you realize that you are not likely to win your superiors' confidence if you take up too much of their time with private problems on such matters as housing, schools, and country clubs. In the discussion you had with representatives of your new company, you probably asked questions about these subjects, so you know exactly how much your management is prepared to help. Use that help as you need it, but don't make unusual or extra demands. And don't try to get special treatment because you have special problems unless you brought up these problems before you took the job and the company agreed to assist you.

Ultimately, you are responsible for your personal affairs. The more they are kept from intruding on your business life, the better you will be able to concentrate on company duties. You were not afraid to make a change in your business life; so don't worry too much about your private life. If you are happy and successful in your job, your family will make out all right even though both you and they will experience some inconveniences before things settle down. Above all, don't let these difficulties detract from your initial efficiency.

An industrial relations executive who lost his position after two years with a new employer was bluntly told, "You are probably a competent labor relations man. The trouble was that you spent practically all of your time during the first year getting your family settled. You didn't have much time left for our work. It got so far beyond you that we lost confidence in your judgment."

The Art of Getting Set—Family Problems

Before writing this book we talked to many executives about the problems involved in changing jobs. All of them emphasized that it is essential to free your mind from personal affairs before beginning a new assignment. An executive from the Worthington Corporation remarked, "It's hard enough to start a new job without sitting around worrying about whether your wife is happy or whether the kids will get along all right in the new school."

If you exercise as much foresight in your private life as you obviously do in business, you and your family began to make plans on how best to accommodate yourselves to the coming change in your lives as soon as it became a probability that you would accept another job. If your new assignment takes you to a different city and area, you learned all you could about what it would be like to live in this new environment. Perhaps you sent your wife on a scouting trip to get straight facts on living conditions and costs. If these costs are higher than they are where you presently live, you probably brought this up during your negotiations for the job, and the cost of living increase is reflected in your salary.

Guide to Getting Established in a New Community

Obviously, it will be ideal if you can get your family installed in their new home before you start work. If you are lucky enough to succeed in doing this, you are in a position to use the interim days between your departure from your old job and your first morning in the new one in getting acclimated to the community which will become your home. What should you do? Here are some suggestions:

1. Visit the school where your children will go, and get acquainted with the teachers.

2. Find a church, if you are a churchgoer, and introduce yourself to the minister. He may be able to offer you good advice in many areas.
3. Learn what attractions the community provides: museums, art galleries, libraries, theaters, recreation centers.
4. Discover what recreational activities the community offers to your children so they can make friends quickly and get over any "homesickness."
5. Go with your wife on an inspection tour of the town. Get acquainted with the right stores, the best and most convenient shopping centers. The happier you can make your wife by helping her solve her problems, the happier she will make you on your job. You need her support; so give her yours.
6. Find out what bank is most convenient for your use and place your accounts there—savings and checking. This will help you to establish local credit quickly.
7. Prepare a list of charge accounts you had in your former town. Get letters of credit reference from some of the merchants with whom you did business.
8. Try to fit into the community as rapidly as possible. Whatever you do, don't make invidious comparisons between your new home and the place where you formerly lived. You moved to the community of your own free will. No town likes to have newcomers point out its faults.
9. If you belong to any social groups or clubs which have branches or chapters in your new community, drop by and get acquainted. The sooner you find yourself at home outside working hours, the easier it will be for you to feel at home on your new job.
10. Learn what activities the community sponsors to

welcome new arrivals: Newcomer's Club, Welcome Wagon, and the like.

Some Tips on Finding a New Home

In most cases when an executive changes both job and location, he is the first to arrive. His children may be in school, and it is desirable for them to complete the term before entering a new school. Furthermore, the old house must no doubt be sold or rented before a new house can be bought. This may mean that the wife must stay behind to attend to "pack up" details. In such a situation, it is not unusual for the company to pay the expenses of the new executive while he is looking around for a place where he and his family can live.

So, if you are at a hotel or a private club and your new management is picking up the bill until you get located, how do you go about finding a new home? Here are some ideas.

If someone else can do the "home hunting" leg work—your wife, a grown daughter—let her. Your job is at the office. Moreover, selecting a good home (within your means) is really your wife's job anyway. It may help if you send her local newspapers and the names of reputable real estate dealers so she can make full and efficient use of her time when she visits you to go house hunting. However, you probably have already learned what sections of town are desirable. This kind of information makes your wife's work easier.

Whether or not you will live in the same neighborhood with other company executives depends on the size of the city to which you are moving, the traditions of the management, and your own personal inclinations.

"I try to live as far away as possible from business associates," said a utility executive, "because I don't want my social life to be a continuation of my business life. Also, I

think after-hours socializing—and this involves wives—
leads to company politics, the growth of cliques, and, frequently, ill feeling between men who should be working
together."

This is an extreme point of view, but on the whole it
makes good sense. Socializing with office associates should
be done in moderation unless you want to become narrow
in your outlook. However, if you are moving to a small
community, you may have little choice as to which neighborhood you will live in. It may all be one.

In the long run, if you do an effective job, it will make
little difference to your management how you conduct
your private affairs—so long as you are circumspect and
do not do anything that reflects discredit on the company.
However—and this is no preachment for conformity—use
care and judgment in choosing your home. Aside from the
fact that it is common sense to live in a neighborhood that
is in line with your standing in the community, your business judgment is at stake.

A personnel man who moved to a town in upper New
York State was criticized by his new associates because he
bought a charming house in a neighborhood that was
going to seed. "He thinks he got a bargain because he got
a big house cheap," remarked a colleague. "But unless he's
planning to go into the funeral-parlor business, he will
never be able to unload it. I hope he gets us better bar-
gains when he negotiates our union contract."

In all probability your new job has brought you a substantial increase in income. You will have extra dollars,
and you will feel exhilaratingly flush. The exhilaration will
not last long. Before you move too fast in buying a home,
remember that you will have more expenses and much
higher taxes. A cloth coat may have been good enough
for your wife last year, but now, in your new position,
nothing less than a fur will do. Be careful about incurring
obligations that may force you to live beyond your income.

A sales manager who moved from Pennsylvania to a New York City job quickly purchased a new house in a highly fashionable commuting town. "I thought I could sell my old home right away and at a profit," he said sadly some time later, "but real estate isn't moving in my neighborhood in Philadelphia. Today I own two houses—one of them empty. The longer the old house stands vacant, the harder it will be to sell. I have reduced the price twice, and not a nibble. I'm dead broke."

Most executives who commented on the housing problem believe, "It's best to sell the old house before you buy the new one. That 'good buy' that's available right now will probably be around when you have gotten your old house off your hands. If it's not—and you have the cash— you will find another house just as good as the one that got away."

These executives also think it wise to leave the family behind until the house is sold, if that is possible. It's hard on the man who is "baching it" and not pleasant for his family either. But it's not forever. If you have your wife back home prodding the real estate people to get busy and helping to sell prospects on the many fine qualities of your house, you will probably get it off your hands sooner.

Your new company may take your house worries off your mind by buying your home and then reselling it. It may even advance you the money to buy a new house. How much an employer will do depends on his policy— or how much he wants to acquire your services. Companies which become deeply involved in the real estate problems of their management personnel are relatively few; they usually are large national manufacturers that have the constant problem of shifting executives around and a real estate department capable of dealing with such matters.

By and large, the average company prefers not to become owner and broker for employee properties. Even so, it may be of real help to you in solving this problem. Thompson-Ramo-Wooldridge, for example, maintains a file of reputable real estate agents. A Philadelphia company assists its managerial people through its real estate department. These instances are typical of the kind of help many employers offer.

A vice president of a manufacturing company commented that when he first reported to work, an associate drove him through several desirable neighborhoods where good homes were available. "I even was worked into a car pool on my second day with the company," he said. Then he paused briefly. "It was certainly a fast way to learn about the company—and the community."

You probably discovered exactly what you could expect from your new employer in the way of housing help before you accepted his offer. If you are a family man, housing is your first major personal consideration. If your wife and family don't like their home, it will be difficult for you to make a go of your job. An industrial relations executive's career was temporarily shattered because he abruptly moved his wife from New York to a small Midwestern town. "I never could convince her that the place was free from Indians," he sadly confessed later, "so I had to look around for another job."

In the final analysis, the responsibility for selecting a home and getting settled in it is yours—not the company's. You are wise if you negotiate the best housing deal possible before you accept the new job. You are even wiser if you make as sure as you can that you will really be happy before you move to an entirely different part of the country simply because you have been offered what seems like a better and more highly paid position.

Although it is very important to acquire permanent or semipermanent living quarters as soon as possible, it is also important to get temporarily "settled down" with equal promptness. If you are ensconced in a good hotel at the company's expense while you look around, don't wear out your welcome. Those living-expense bills will look bigger and bigger to your boss as they pile up.

Should You Rent or Buy?

Many executives think it is better to rent before buying even if getting rid of your old home is no problem. This gives you time to look around and get exactly what you want. Besides, if the new job doesn't work out, you'll find out in a year or so. Getting rid of an apartment is much simpler than trying to unload a house.

"The man who hired me was kind enough to rent temporary quarters for me and my family," said the traffic manager of a paper company. "This apartment was quite satisfactory for a temporary home. It kept us 'loose' so we could shop around."

A university professor, transferring from one school to another, solved his housing dilemma by calling an associate in his field and introducing himself. "We have never met," he began, "but I know you by reputation. I am joining the faculty of your college, and I am wondering about rentals." He got the full story and several good leads. Quite casually he telephoned one of these leads and made arrangements to rent a furnished apartment until he could find something more permanent.

Industry itself is something of a fraternity. Undoubtedly you have met executives from many parts of the country at conventions, seminars, or conferences. If you want straight information about the housing situation in the community where you will soon live, call a colleague at a company that is located there. He will probably talk straight from the shoulder. Since he is not an employee of your new company, he has no reason to try and paint a bright picture of what to expect.

How serious your housing problem will be depends on

the type of community in which you will live. A large New Jersey company goes all out to help its employees get settled in the complex metropolitan area where its headquarters plant is located. It has careful discussions on housing with executives whom it hires before it lets them make the change. Real estate help is offered through agents, and also personal help. The company doesn't want to have an unhappily housed executive on its staff or to have a man suffer a real estate loss because he accepted a position with it.

What About Moving Expenses?

It's expensive to move your household from one community to another. In all probability, the cost of living was one of the subjects you discussed when you were considering the new job. Very likely your new employer agreed to reimburse you for all, or at least part, of this expense. However, the move will still cost you money. Items you have never thought about will come up to drain cash from the bank account.

"My company agreed to pay my moving expenses, and it did," moaned a recently transferred sales executive, "but I figure I'm still out of pocket about $1,000. There are so many things that run up the price of moving, and most of them I couldn't legitimately charge to the company."

When this executive used the word "legitimately," he touched on an important subject. If your company is footing the bill, don't hit it with everything but the kitchen sink. Your new management has a fairly precise idea of what it costs to move from one place to another. If your bill is sky-high because you included a great many unusual or non-job-related expenses, you won't make a good impression. Your new employer may even question your bill, and that will be embarrassing. If he grits his teeth and pays it, he may still wonder if you are trying to make money out of your transfer.

"Keep an eye on that fellow's expense account," one executive vice president warned the company controller after he reviewed the moving expenses of a public relations executive who had just been hired. "If this bill is any sample, he spends money as though it were going out of style."

When you have decided to take another job and your prospective employer has agreed to pay your moving expenses, get accurate estimates on how much they will be. Submit these to your new company before you make the move. That way you will have advance approval of your expenditures, and there will be no criticism regarding the amount of the bill.

About Hospitalization, Insurance, and Pensions

After you have solved your housing problems, check up on how soon you will be covered at your new company by hospitalization, health, and welfare programs. Don't assume anything. You don't want to discover, after either you or some member of your family gets sick, that the heavy medical bills you thought would be paid for by the insurance company are headed straight for your pocketbook. Your new employer may have a fine benefit program, but it may not cover you automatically on the first day you go to work. At many firms, employees (including executives) must wait as long as three months before they are eligible to participate in company insurance, health, and welfare benefits.

Before accepting a job at a certain company, an executive inquired of his prospective employer, "Do you have a comprehensive health and welfare plan for management people?" He was assured that the program was as good as the one he was giving up, and the literature describing it justified the assurance. "When will I be covered?" he asked. "On the first day of the first month after you report to work. You report on December 31; so you will be covered on January 1," was the reply.

The executive dismissed the matter from his mind. Unfortunately, private business caused him to request a delay in his starting date until January 15. It was granted. The man reported on January 15, and exactly one week later he had a severe heart attack. His wife learned the sad news. Her husband would not become eligible for the company's health and welfare protection until February 1. Worst of all, the protection from his old medical insurance program, which he could have extended by paying the bills himself, had lapsed.

Most companies where an employee has been paying premiums for several years will allow him to continue his insurance and medical benefits, at least for a reasonable period of time, if he picks up the tab himself. This is certainly true of Blue Cross. But it is usually up to the individual to make the arrangements. Also, the details of company insurance programs differ.

A large New England electrical company paid full insurance benefits for a vice president who died the second day after he had assumed his post. This executive had insisted that he be covered by all of the company's insurance programs the first day he was on the job and would take the position on no other terms. The company wanted him badly enough to make these concessions. However, this is not always the case. Some companies will pay insurance benefits to a man who dies the second day he is on the job; on the other hand, the employee who quits must arrange for his own coverage.

Your pension rights are another item to investigate. Unless you have acquired vested rights in your company's program, usually you lose your benefits—with the exception of the portion you have contributed—when you leave one company to accept a job elsewhere.

Many realistic management people assume that unless an ambitious younger executive attains promotion at his own company within three to five years, he will probably seek greener pastures. Since most pension plans do not vest until a person has been covered for at least five, and more usually ten, years, the matter of pensions is of vital interest to an increasingly transient executive population which realizes the importance of building up an income for one's old age. Therefore, many management men who get back their contributions to a company pension plan because they are resigning count this cash as savings. They invest it in annuities or some other type of saving plan so that they do not entirely lose the retirement protection they have established for themselves and their families.

If you have been foresighted, you have considered any benefit losses you would incur in leaving your old firm to go to another company. In fact, you accepted the new job because you decided that in balance you would gain financially. Whenever you give up one job to take another, you probably lose something, but you can't have your cake and eat it too. If you are so security-conscious that you shudder at the prospect of relinquishing one company's pension and insurance benefits to take a better job with more money at another, you are wise to stay on the job you have and forget about other possibilities. They will only frustrate you and make you unhappy because you are afraid to take the risk. Your new benefit plan will probably be as good as the old one as soon as you have acquired sufficient service to be covered by it. Furthermore, in a year or so your increased income and wider opportunities will more than offset any losses you may have sustained.

Nobody can see into the future. A 49-year-old railroad executive turned down an excellent job with an insurance company some years ago because he thought he could not afford to give up his pension investment. However, when he reached 62 his company instituted a forced retirement program, and he found himself on the shelf with a greatly reduced pension, speculating on the keen insight John Greenleaf Whittier showed when he wrote that the saddest words of tongue or pen are these: "It might have been."

Whatever you do, don't bore your new associates by telling them how much pension money you lost because you gave up your old job. They don't care. They hired you to think about your career, not about your retirement.

Many companies offer investment help to new executives. Perhaps you can get assistance from some expert on your new employer's financial staff if you don't know how best to invest monies you have received from your pension contributions or other benefit programs of your last company. When you have settled down in your job and gotten the duties of your new position well under your belt will be time enough to take care of personal matters of this kind. At the beginning, so far as possible, your new job should be your main concern.

What to Do About Outside Interests

If you have an outside business or do consulting work on the side, it is important that you explain this clearly to your future employer. Why risk trouble later because you thought it best to let sleeping dogs lie? Your former company may not have minded, but you never know how your new boss will view such activities until you ask him. His company may have hard-and-fast policies forbidding an executive to be associated with any extracurricular activity that might be considered a conflict of interest. During the negotiations for your job you should have discussed such matters carefully. Your new employer may allow you to continue your outside work, or he may tell you that you will have to give up anything that is not job-connected. If he does object to your outside activities, he will certainly give you sufficient time to relinquish such interests without loss.

Don't make the mistake of keeping quiet about some profitable sideline. One executive who evidently believed that what his future boss didn't know wouldn't hurt him neglected to mention that he was an active partner in an engineering consulting firm. He was called on the carpet when the president of his company discovered this association.

"But you never told me specifically that my outside work was against company policy," the executive complained. "You never asked," retorted the president, "so you must have thought it best not to. I don't think you have been very honest in this matter, and I don't like officers I can't trust. I think we will both be better off if I give you your freedom so you can concentrate on your business."

You want a clear understanding with your company on every subject that relates to your job. The time to have this meeting of minds is before you begin work.

The Importance of Being Well Dressed

Advance planning is the hallmark of the good executive, and this applies even to the "get ready" period before you start a new assignment. You want to swing into your new duties with as little lost motion as possible. Very soon you will be moving into your new office, and there will be new problems to solve, new associates to meet and know, new challenges, new risks, new triumphs and disappointments. The months ahead will be exciting and stimulating.

It will all start when you walk into the reception hall of your new company and give your name to the girl at the desk. She is expecting you and has been wondering what you look like. "Mr. Jones is here," she will report, sizing you up with cautious curiosity. "Shall I send him up?" Within minutes your new boss will be shaking your hand. The receptionist? Her telephone will be busy as she tells her friends, "Yes, he's arrived. Well, not exactly handsome, but still good looking—and not too old. I wonder if he's married?"

Everybody knows you are coming—your associates, the clerks, the stenographers, the secretaries. They want to know all about you. Are you married? How many children have you? What's your personality like? You will have every eye on you. So dress properly, for good grooming is important.

John D. Rockefeller was once criticized by a friend for walking to his New York office in a very seedy business suit. "But everybody knows who I am," explained Rockefeller, "so it doesn't matter." When, some time later, the same friend saw Rockefeller in Boston, he was wearing the same clothes. Again the friend suggested that he should be better dressed. "But nobody knows who I am in Boston," said Rockefeller, "so what does it matter?"

You aren't Rockefeller, and everybody knows who you are at your new company. That is knowledge which you don't share about the others. Only the rare eccentric whose abilities have been firmly established has won the right to be offbeat in his appearance. You don't have to be a fashion plate, but it is common sense to dress conservatively for your first entrance on the scene of your new job. It's also wise to eschew gaudy or unusual appurtenances in clothing or accessories—until you get set in your work and know your way around. An advertising executive who wore dark glasses his first day on the job learned later that the story had spread that he was covering up a hangover. A new purchasing executive offended a perhaps too fastidious superior because he had a colored handkerchief in his breast pocket.

How to Get Ready for Your Induction

"Be sure to get a good night's sleep before you report to a new job," advises Joseph McIntosh, director of industrial relations for the American Gas Company. The emotional strain of a new assignment is hard to measure. Furthermore, you are showing foresight if you prepare yourself mentally for unforeseen emergencies or difficulties that might come up the first day.

A manufacturing executive tells of an embarrassing incident that occurred when he went to work for a different firm. "I was so excited the night before that I didn't get a wink of sleep. The next afternoon, when my new boss dropped by my office for further discussions about my job, I was dozing."

Another man tells this story: "I thought I had been filled in on everything, but I forgot to ask where to report. I knew my office would be at the plant, but I assumed I should see my boss in his office at the company's headquarters downtown. I arrived there to find nobody knew anything about me. My boss was waiting at the plant to show me around. He laughed about the incident, but I still think I got started on the wrong foot."

To ask where you are to report seems almost elementary. But the nervous strain of starting a new career may make you forget many basic and routine questions. You—and sometimes others—are likely to worry over the trivial errors you make during your first two or three days on the job and magnify them out of all proportion to their importance. This is foolish. You are trying hard to impress relative strangers with your poise and confidence; so do your best to anticipate any difficulties that would put you in a bad light. However, if you do make a mistake, don't fret. The best thing to do is to act natural.

One experienced executive advises: "Before you report

to a new job make a checklist. It should include such items as where you are to report, when you are to report, how you get to the plant or office, where you park your car, the names and titles of executives you have met during your pre-job interviews. Don't rely on memory. Write down this information in your notebook and you can't go wrong."

Learn all you can about the company's policies and organizational setup before you report to work. During discussions with the executives who offered the job, you were told the general organizational pattern of the corporation and something about its key policies. But before you begin your assignment, try to study these in detail. Ask your future employer to supply you with company organizational charts, employee and supervisory manuals, policy manuals, and similar literature. Many executives kill the first days on new assignments by reviewing information of this kind. If you have such facts at your fingertips before you start, you are just that much further ahead. You are prepared to ask intelligent questions on all subjects that you do not fully understand.

Punctuality is most important. Be sure you know what time the office opens and what time it is customary for your new superior to be at his desk. Plan to arrive 15 minutes to half an hour later. You should give him sufficient time to get settled and make arrangements for your welcome. But don't keep him waiting so long that he begins to wonder where you are.

An executive from an oil company says: "When you start that new job, it will probably be on a Monday. Use the preceding Saturday or Sunday for a dry run on how to get to the office quickly. On the day I came to work here, I drove. It was a mistake. Our office is in the middle of town. I couldn't find a nearby parking lot, and by the time I got my car parked and made it back to the office, I was an hour and a half late. Had I done any advance planning, I would have taken a bus."

You can expect your superior or one of your new associates to take you on a tour of the offices or plant during your first day on the job. At this time you will meet the people with whom you will work. In fact, depending on the friendliness of your relationship with your new boss, you may even suggest such a tour if he forgets. He also has much on his mind and is under pressure. He wants to make a good impression on you, and he wants you to like the organization. In his anxiety to get you started right, he may overlook one or two details. Don't let it bother you. It is not deliberate.

When you arrive at your new office, you should be as relaxed as possible. Don't let the general curiosity about you get you down. You want people's approval, so of course you will be pleasant and friendly. But be prepared to keep your mouth shut and listen, listen, listen. A newly appointed public relations vice president made such a poor impression on his associates at an old-line, conservative utility company that he was never able to overcome it. He dominated conversations with every executive he met during his first days at the firm. He had no hesitation in telling how "we got things done at my old shop" and how things could be improved at the new one. He lasted less than two years.

Be careful about assuming close relationships with associates too quickly. You may pick the wrong horse. As a noted management consultant has observed, "Don't be fooled by an organizational chart. The most sacrosanct organizational chart that includes the most logical reporting steps may turn out to be a river a mile long and an inch deep. Everybody really reports to one man; and if you are in his bad books, you lose out no matter what your boss thinks." So do your best to keep an open and objective mind. Let experience confirm the statements you have read in company policy and organizational manuals. That way, you won't act prematurely and impose needless handicaps on yourself right at the start.

Study Your Environment

"It's good business to learn as much as you can about the political climate of a company before you start work," declared a seasoned executive at a well-known national company. "Just because you are a Republican, and businessmen are supposed to be Republicans, don't assume all of them are. You may make a faux pas if you come up with some smart cracks about the mess in Washington only to find that the people you are talking to are staunch supporters of the Administration."

The same thing goes for religion. A somewhat meticulous financial executive, new on his job, advised his secretary to wash her face when he noticed ashes on her forehead on a certain winter Wednesday. "Look around you, sir," she snapped, "and you'll notice that there are many dirty faces here today. The president of our company is also Catholic." A nominal Protestant, the executive simply had not realized it was Ash Wednesday.

Your first day at the office will largely be confined to getting acquainted. Your superior and probably some of your new associates will take you to lunch. In your advance planning you should count on it. You should have sufficient sensitivity to judge very quickly whether or not you are expected to take a drink if it is offered. Teetotal it or take only one is good advice. It is amazing how quickly a rumor gets started that an executive drinks too much. However, an assistant sales manager at a Texas paper company got the reputation of being somewhat of a prude because he refused to take a drink at a convivial welcoming luncheon his new superior had arranged. He had no objection to a cocktail—even at lunch. He was simply trying too hard to make a good impression. Your sensitivity to the situation and to people is your best guide on what to do. But if you don't know or are uncertain, just ask your boss. He will understand.

Stay within time limits at lunch, at least until you know your way around and have learned company customs. Nothing upsets a boss so much as to ask where a new subordinate is and be told, "He's still at lunch." You don't want to create an initial impression that you are the kind of person "who arrives late at work and makes up for it by going home early."

Don't Be Upset by Temporary Inconveniences

The first day on your new job will be a strain, even though you may not notice it until you go home that night. For example, your permanent office may not be ready and it may be necessary for you to accept temporary quarters. Don't be upset, and don't argue about accommodations when you know perfectly well they will soon be improved. On the other hand, don't be a softie. Make your superior understand, without being belligerent or bad-humored, that you expect an office commensurate with your rank. If you indicate that you will put up with anything, you may find yourself working for the man you have been brought in to supersede.

An executive who had been hired to take charge of industrial relations at a certain company was told that the man he was replacing would retain the title and be kept on the staff for three more months. "However, the day you come in you are boss and entitled to occupy the vice president's office" was the promise. When this executive reported to work, he found that the office into which he had expected to move was still occupied by its former tenant. "I'm sure," he was told by his soon-to-leave associate, "that you won't mind using this small office for a short time. I simply haven't had time to get my books and papers packed."

The new executive realized that his predecessor intended to stay put in his old office until his termination date. He had known when his replacement was coming for at least six weeks. The new executive said nothing—the first day. The next morning he told his associate, "I'm expecting several visitors today, and I will need my office when they come. The one I'm now using isn't large enough. I will let you know when they leave so you can go back. You're welcome to use the office until you finish packing your books and papers, but when people come to see me I must talk to them in my regular office. I'm sure you will understand. It won't be much of a problem, for I suppose you will be out by the weekend."

Had the new executive let things slide, he would have sat in the small office until the former department head finally departed. Certainly he would have lost face with his subordinates. They had realized that their old boss was trying to hang onto his quarters, and were wondering whether the new man would let him get away with it.

Situations of this kind come up more frequently than you may think. They require tactful but firm handling. If you can cope with them yourself, you will demonstrate initiative and resourcefulness. The executive mentioned above could have gone to his superiors and forced the issue. But that would have created a hullabaloo, which is the last thing you want when you start a new job.

What About Bringing in Your Old Team?

During negotiations with your new employer, it may have been possible for you to arrange to bring your former secretary and one or two key people with you. If so, well and good, but it is best not to be too hasty. There is nothing more upsetting to a department's morale than to have a new team move in all at once and take over lock, stock, and barrel. Even a poorly run organization has many capable people. Furthermore, you have to depend on employees already on the job to learn the ropes. Even a company that is being reshuffled needs a sense of continuity. If you are the kind of new broom that sweeps so clean that you replace everybody, you will have no roots. In such a case, you will make many mistakes that you could have avoided had you retained some old hands to advise you. So, if you plan to bring in new people, do it slowly and don't overdo it.

Whatever you do, limit the number of people you take from your former employer. You may invite one or two key men who have worked for you over the years and who, you consider, are your team. But you have an obligation to your old company. It gave you the opportunity that earned you your present job. Don't rob it blind of its good men. Your first job is to win the loyalty and confidence of your new subordinates. They will like you better if they see that you have not prejudged them and intend to give them every chance to prove their capabilities.

Finally, if you have inherited a good secretary, you may have gotten a real break. Provided she is flexible enough to transfer her loyalties to you, she can be invaluable in getting you started right—if you let her. In every company there are traditions and customs that executives observe. Here is where your secretary can be of great assistance. You need someone who can answer questions that you would hesitate to ask a superior or an associate.

An executive who had just taken a job with a very conservative company remarked, "My secretary saved me considerable embarrassment my first day on the job. She noticed I was wearing a bow tie and told me, 'I hope you don't think I'm impertinent, but here top officers simply don't wear bow ties. I know you are meeting the president this afternoon for the first time, so I took the liberty of buying you a four-in-hand.'"

You will have to make sharp judgments about your new subordinates, but that is for the future. On your first days keep an open mind. The advice of associates from other departments regarding your people may be helpful, but it also may be misleading. The man who was considered a marginal performer when he worked for your predecessor may take a new lease on life under you if you give him a start-from-scratch opportunity and the right kind of leadership.

Your Obligations to Your Past Employer

Although you have severed connections with your old company, you may still have obligations to it—an incompleted project or an assignment which your former management had counted on you to finish. Don't let it down. If there are any matters of this kind still up in the air at the time you are supposed to report to your new company, explain the situation to your new superiors and ask them for permission to wind up all of your affairs.

"When I reported to work as personnel director of my company," said an ex-job-and-salary-rating expert of the National Metal Trades Association, "I explained to my boss that I was morally obligated to return to a company where I had installed NMTA's job-rating system to do a two-day recheck. It was scheduled for two months after the date on which I took over my new job. My boss understood and gladly gave me permission to go."

Unless you want to be known as an opportunist, you must be conscientious in fulfilling all commitments you have made to your former employer. Your new management will respect you for this and cooperate with you. It shouldn't be too much of a problem. When you named the day you would start your new job, you probably gave yourself sufficient time to tie down all the loose ends of your former assignment. If this wrap-up takes longer than you anticipated, don't hesitate to let your new company know. Ask your prospective superior's help in finding ways to solve the problem. Your new company doesn't want bad relations with your former employer because of you. And you certainly would like to have the goodwill of your old company. You enjoyed working there, and you still wish it well. Some day you may need its good opinion.

Summary Checklist: Getting Ready for a New Assignment

The following checklist may be of assistance in making sure you have overlooked no detail in getting ready to begin a new and broader phase of your business career.

1. *Plan your approach.* Your new job is a responsibility that it is up to you to handle. Be sure you cause your new employer as little difficulty as possible.

2. *Take care of as many items of personal business as you can before you begin work.* You don't want your private affairs to intrude on your business time during the important first weeks of your new assignment.

3. *Help your family make the change.* It is most important for them and for you to adjust quickly and smoothly to a new environment.

4. *Review your total insurance program.* Make sure you are covered for life, sickness and accident, hospitalization, and disaster during the transition period between leaving one job and taking another.

5. *Study all the manuals in use in your new company.* The more you know about the organization, policies, practices, and products of your future company before you start, the better off you will be.

6. *Straighten out your outside activities.* If you are connected with a project that you must discontinue, begin immediately to withdraw from it.

7. *Be prepared to listen and learn.* It's always wise to show that you're willing to learn before you start to teach.

8. *Go slow in telling how things were done where you last worked.* Nobody likes to be on the short end of a newcomer's comparisons.

9. *Never criticize your past management,* not even if this criticism is deserved.

10. *Take your time about bringing your old team with you.* Plan to evaluate your new subordinates and, if they have abilities, give them every opportunity. They deserve it for the years they have invested in the company. Your job is to win their loyalty and trust.

11. *Learn about the customs of the company before you start work.* Knowledge of this kind may save you from face-flushing initial bloopers.

12. *Don't wear a chip for an epaulette when you start your job.* Neither should you hesitate to assume any assigned authority. Your subordinates and associates will be testing you during your first days. Be friendly but firm. You're entitled to "wait and see," so plan not to get rushed into any premature decisions.

13. *Ask for help.* Most of your associates and probably all of your superiors want you to make good. The advice of competent subordinates may also be helpful.

14. *Get your financial affairs under control.* Don't ask for any unusual concessions—money, time off— unless it's absolutely necessary.

15. *Discuss expenses beforehand.* Don't try to stick your new management for moving, buying a house, or selling an old one unless you have discussed this before taking the job and the company has agreed to help you.

16. *Be well rested.* First impressions are important.
17. *Report on time and at the right place.* Punctuality is a sign of responsibility.
18. *Be well groomed and conservatively dressed.* You don't have to look like an undertaker or a candidate for the list of the country's ten best-groomed men, but dress neatly and inconspicuously when you meet the people who will work with you on your new job.

CHAPTER II

THE FIRST DAYS
ON YOUR NEW JOB

THERE ARE NO SET RULES THAT CAN BE PRESCRIBED TO govern your course of conduct during your first days on a new job. However, there are certain suggestions which may make your breaking-in period easier and more productive.

What you do during the starting weeks on your new assignment depends on the authority and power that are vested in your job. For example, a wage and salary administrator who is brought in to handle this function of his company's operation will face problems totally different from those, say, of a new executive vice president who has been hired to breathe fresh life into a "tired organization." The wage and salary executive's first objective is to sell himself and the services he offers. His is a staff assignment, and he does not usually work from a base of power. On the other hand, the executive vice president has been given definite goals, and on his success may hinge his own survival and that of his company. He must quickly analyze the assets and weaknesses of his employer from the standpoint of product, service, merchandising, and sales. He must also evaluate the ability of the executives charged with these responsibilities and determine what changes, if any, are necessary in management personnel. True, he

may meet resistance from various executives who fear or
resent change, but this resistance is not likely to be overt.
His position assures him of at least lip service. After all,
he's the boss and has the authority to say, "Either my word
goes or the person who opposes it does."

Your Initial Course of Action: Job Factors

When you begin a new job, there are certain factors you
should weigh before charting your initial course. Here
they are:

1. The responsibilities and the authority of the job.
2. The relative importance of the job in your department and in the company as a whole.
3. The importance and influence of your department
   in the company.
4. The influence your department head has with executives in other departments and with top management.
5. The respect with which your department is treated
   by executives in other departments.
6. The backing your department receives from top
   management.
7. The firmness with which your job is fixed in the
   company organizational chart. (Are you succeed-
   ing to a well-established position or to a newly
   created job the need for which has only recently
   been discovered by management?)
8. The support you will receive from your superior in
   carrying out your duties.
9. The attitude of subordinates, particularly key subordinates, one or two of whom may have aspired
   to the position you now have.
10. The nature of the job itself. (Is it line or staff? An
    operational executive will take quite a different
    approach from that of the staff man who has to

convince manufacturing men that they need his
services and, incidentally, should pay the cost of
these services out of their budgets.)

The Importance of Caution

A good general never commits his forces to premature
action. Neither should you. While you can't expect to
acquire an immediate comprehension of the complicated
inner relationships among departments or among executives, you can at least be aware that much exists beneath
the surface—tensions, conflicts of interest, frustrations—
that you don't see. Move cautiously, at least in your deal-
ings with associates, until you get a clear understanding
of the internal power structure. Whatever you do, don't be
impulsive or arrive at faulty conclusions on scanty evidence. This may cause you to commit irretrievable blun-
ders.

A newly appointed public relations director of an Eastern corporation explains how an error of this kind nearly
wrecked his career. "I worked for the parent company,"
he said, "but it was housed in the plant of its largest subsidiary. One vice president of the parent company suggested that we do a local news release on our acquisition
of a plant in a nearby community. I prepared the release,
and it appeared in the local papers. Soon afterward I discovered that I had mortally offended the head of the advertising department of the subsidiary firm. Traditionally,
his people had been responsible for all local publicity. He
assumed that the vice president of the parent company
was trying to take over his duties and using me as a front
man. I later learned that the vice president was on bad
terms with the management of the subsidiary and was in
a very shaky position with his president and other top
executives. Here I was—only two days on my new job
and already caught in the middle of a company row. It

took more than a year to make my peace with the management of the subsidiary."

This incident is typical of what you may encounter in a new assignment if your duties overlap those of another department. People are jealous of their prerogatives and especially resentful toward a newcomer who assumes a responsibility that they have long considered theirs, even if it is not one they particularly want.

Establish Your Authority

The executive whose new assignment comes with built-in authority and responsibility frequently has a more difficult time than does the man who is hired in a subordinate capacity. More is expected of a top management executive, and there is no one to run interference for him. To begin with, it is hard for him to identify sources of opposition. People who work for him are not too likely to come forward with advice, at least until he wins their confidence. Associates at his level have their own worries. Furthermore, they can assume a wait-and-see attitude.

Said the vice president of an aviation company: "I was hired by the president, and he gave me complete backing. But there was one man on my staff who had expected the promotion. He had been with the company many years, and when he was bypassed he was extremely disappointed and bitter. He had the sympathy of many of my associates and some of the key men on my own staff. Fortunately, I had had the foresight to anticipate this problem. The president and I had a clear understanding regarding my authority.

"I soon realized that there was a strong undercurrent of hostility between me and my chief subordinate, and that passively he was resisting my authority. I called him in, and we had a frank talk. I told him honestly that I knew of his disappointment and that I was sorry to be the cause of it. Then I bluntly said that he had two choices: to forget his troubles and buckle down, or to get out. Soon afterward I learned that he had gone over my head to complain to the president. Next day I told him he was being given three months' severance pay and that his duties would be taken over by someone else. This bowled him over, but he still thought he was a fixture and I couldn't make his dismissal stick. I could! After his departure, morale in my department went up. My people knew I meant business. If I have any advice to give a man in the same circumstances it is this: Win your battles early. Be fair and firm, but demonstrate that you're the man in charge."

Another executive describes a similar but happier situation that occurred when he was appointed vice president of a precision instrument company. "The man I succeeded had suffered from a severe heart attack and had been moved into an advisory staff position that involved light duties until he became eligible for his pension. However, my predecessor was a realist. He gave me advice only when I asked for it—and his advice was good. He quickly told me, 'I have been in charge of this division so long that I may be an embarrassment to you, especially when you change my ways of doing things. I propose that you give me an office in the downtown sales building. You can call on me when you need my help, and I won't be in the way. After all, I'll be retiring within a year.'"

Hannibal, the great Carthaginian general, on learning that the Roman army he faced was commanded by two generals with joint responsibility for the conduct of the coming battle, observed that Carthage could not lose. He said, "I have greater fear of one mediocre general who has complete charge of a battle than of two great generals who share authority."

When you take the responsibility for a key job, you must quickly establish your authority. You do not have to do that by bull-in-the-china-shop methods. A wise executive seeks and accepts good advice, but vacillation or hesitancy during your first days may limit your later career, even crowd you off the organization chart. Associates may judge you as lacking in courage. You must make it plain to both subordinates and colleagues that you expect to run the department and will make key policy decisions affecting it. However, to win their confidence and goodwill, you must also show that you need and want their suggestions and recommendations. Never assert your authority simply because you are boss. A wise leader delays action until he is reasonably sure of the proper move. But there is a difference between sitting still and studying a situation and simply sitting still because you're waiting for someone to tell you what to do.

How to Size Up Subordinates Initially

When you begin a new top management job, you will have to make some curbstone judgments of the people who report to you. The organization chart outlines their responsibilities, and you have probably been given some advance information as to the abilities and characteristics of certain of the key people. This information may be useful, but don't accept it literally or allow it to prejudice your judgments. It may not be entirely accurate. No doubt it came from other executives, and their judgments may not have been made at first hand.

"The president of my firm gave me a detailed account of all the department heads who would report to me," said a manufacturing vice president, "and he was honest in his evaluations. But he had gained most of his impressions from my retired predecessor, a man who absolutely refused to delegate. The president had been told that certain of my subordinates were capable but showed a surprising lack of initiative; that others were good but required close supervision because they tended to go off half-cocked.

Had I judged my subordinates on the basis of the president's information, I would have lost some of my best men. I soon discovered that the men who I had been told 'tended to go off half-cocked' were topnotch. They had chafed under the rigid discipline of my predecessor, and several of them would have left the company had they not known he was slated for retirement. I gave my people the authority which—on paper—they already had, and they developed rapidly."

"Keep your mind open and your mouth shut while you are analyzing the competence of subordinates and deciding where and how they will best fit in your future plans," observed a successful sales executive. "You have plenty of time to judge them. The first thing to do is to learn the details of their various jobs, and then you can decide by observation and follow-through the initiative and competence they are showing."

It is seldom a mistake to go slow—at least as slow as circumstances permit—during the early stages of a new career. Your very presence on the payroll has had its impact on subordinates. You represent change, and they are waiting to see how this change will affect them. Understandably, they are insecure and uncertain. The more quickly you take hold and re-establish their confidence in themselves, the more surely you can move forward.

A successful industrialist commented that within a week after he had been named president of a Midwestern company he interviewed each of his chief subordinates to learn the precise nature of their responsibilities. "I asked each man to bring his principal assistants with him," he continued, "because I had brought two of my people with me. I didn't want these department heads to have to explain their duties to me and later do it all over again for the two men I was bringing to the organization. Anything you can do to speed the settling-down process is helpful."

Every organization needs a shake-up now and again, but

it should be a controlled process if you expect the chips to fall in the right pattern. If your entrance into a new management is accompanied by loud alarums and the fatuous fanfare of needless sound and fury, communication barriers are built up between yourself and the people you must depend upon.

A young researcher at a large management consulting firm, in describing the effect that a highly publicized shake-up had on rank-and-file employees, said: "Although in the long run nothing much happened to most of us, our new boss spent so much time trumpeting about coming changes that we all expected to lose our jobs. We spent the first six weeks he was here listening to rumors, and that made us very uncertain. Many of us began looking for other jobs. However, after a few months our boss learned that it takes time to make changes. Furthermore, he didn't help himself with associates in other departments when he began to lose so many good people."

Beware of Entangling Alliances

It is wise to move slowly in identifying yourself with individual associates or even with particular groups of your colleagues. Remarked an industrial relations man: "When I became personnel vice president of my company, the financial vice president was especially nice to me. I didn't realize he was cultivating my friendship so that I would become an ally in his campaign to have plant controllers in each unit of the company report directly to him instead of to the plant manager. The cold reception that the manufacturing vice president gave to all of my plans, and his criticism of my department, made me talk to him to find out why. He said, 'You picked your side the day you came to our company. You'd better be certain it's the right side, because if it's not you won't last long.'"

In your position you have influence and authority. While

the colleague who courts your favor is probably sincere and anxious to help, there is just an outside chance that his motive is self-serving. It does you no harm to be friendly, but it's also wise to avoid early commitments. You are still an outsider and are supposed to be an expert. Furthermore, you are so new to the company that you are expected to look at its problems objectively. If a particular associate (or group of colleagues) is successful in enlisting your premature assistance in advancing some pet project, that may tip the scale in his favor. It may also earn you the lasting resentment of other executives who think that you made up your mind not on the merits of the case but on its politics.

You don't want this to happen. Luckily, your very newness gives you protection. No reasonable person can object when a new executive refuses to express an opinion about a company plan of action or policy until he has had both the time and the experience to examine it properly.

Use the first weeks to make friends on a broad basis throughout the company. You have no bone to pick with anybody. If you can demonstrate that you came to do a job and that you expect to accomplish it through the merit of your recommendations and programs—not through politics—you may not win everybody's friendship, but you will win respect for your integrity. Inevitably, there will be clashes with associates whose interests or ideas conflict with yours. If possible, defer such clashes until you are well established and have sufficient experience with the company to defend your views within the framework of actual facts based on specific company problems, not on emotion or generalities. The more successful you are in avoiding personalities in business differences, the better you are able to perform your duties.

"A good top executive must learn to accept the best from many conflicting ideas," said the president of a well-known chemical company, "and he is wise if he learns to adjust to various types of people. He doesn't do this by being all things to all men. He does it by being himself to everybody and by showing that his advocacy of a course of action is based on his analysis of the facts and not his friendship with its proponents."

Problems of the Staff Executive

The staff executive, even at the vice-presidential level, has to overcome problems that are different from those of the line officer. His function is to provide a service. His power derives from his superiors in top management and not from the profit-making ability of his own department. "Remember you are part of overhead," a seasoned staff vice president warns, "and that your services are paid for by line activities. The minute you begin to build an empire and allow your costs to exceed the value of the assistance you provide, you are in trouble."

An industrial relations man cautioned a young assistant that his main job was to "sell" line people that the help he offered was needed. "The plant manager may be wrong in turning down your training program," he said, "but it's up to you to wait for another opportunity and try again. Don't get into arguments with him and attempt to prove him wrong. We're riding on his budget. If the vice president of manufacturing gets into an argument with the vice president of sales, he is likely to lose it. And if the vice president of industrial relations gets into an argument with either one of them, he is almost sure to lose."

Many staff people, particularly if they have been hired to head up newly established departments such as public relations or even personnel, have been bitterly disappointed at the reception they have received at their new companies. Said the hardbitten production chief of a medium-size manufacturing company to an industrial relations executive who had been induced to join the management to establish such a department: "Your project is the president's baby. We need it like a hole in the head. We were getting along all right before you came, and we'll do okay when you're gone. Play up to the president and you'll be all right—so long as he's on this kick. But don't come snooping around our department with human relations programs and things like that. We have work to do."

Another executive recounts an occasion when he turned down the vice presidency of industrial relations at a Midwestern aluminum company. "The consulting firm had really built up the job," he said, "and the president was most enthusiastic. But I soon discovered that my job was intended to be an advisory one—to the president. Each plant was to continue to run its own industrial relations program, especially labor relations, through its own plant manager. My function would be to advise the president on how well they were doing and give him and the top staff my ideas on how things could be improved. I was to have no direct contact with the plant managers.

"The company was family-owned. The president was 63 years old, and the desire to create the job he offered me was strictly his. In talking to his subordinates, particularly operating people, I soon sensed that they were not at all enthusiastic about my department but did not want to oppose it openly. Had I taken the position I would have been like a golf ball on a tee. When the president retired, I would be a setup to get knocked off. An acquaintance of mine took the job and lasted 18 months. That was two months past the date the president retired."

When you are new with a company, the main thing to do is to keep your balance. If you are mature, you can still be an expert and not rub oldtimers the wrong way.

When Lawrence Stessin was vice president of the National Foreman's Institute, he told of a writer who was hired for a staff editorial position. "The man had zip and smartness, but he didn't understand how to move into a new job with finesse. Partly because his boss shoved him down everybody's throat and partly because of his own know-it-all attitude, he didn't really have a chance. The resentment he built up defeated him. He came to me and asked whether or not he should leave. I said he should go because he had incurred so much ill will that he would have difficulty accomplishing his assignment. However, he has learned his lesson. He took another job and has done well ever since."

Learn Your New Assignment by Working at It

No matter how thorough you have been in your pre-job investigations, you won't get the true picture of your assignment until you are actually working at it. This is true whether your job is line or staff. But if you are an operational executive, you deal in specifics. It's always easier to orient yourself to a new environment if the assignment you are undertaking is technical and tangible. The staff executive, on the other hand, even though the services he provides are technical in nature, still is in the position of the salesman who must convince the customer that he has a good, solid product.

"If I have any advice to give a staff man starting a new job, it is this," said a seasoned industrial relations executive. "Use the first weeks—that's the honeymoon—getting to know the top department heads whose cooperation is essential to your success. Learn what their problems are, and be sensitive to their attitudes. Don't overwhelm them with ideas. Let them do the talking first. Impress on them that you are cost-conscious and practical. Before you announce any new programs or describe the different directions that you expect to follow, make sure you have considered their suggestions; and when they fit in with your views, accept them and give credit. Don't criticize or be-

little past practices or methods. You never know who
originated them. And whatever you do at the very beginning, don't outline a broadly ambitious program in detail.
Most people are afraid of revolutionaries. Listen and learn,
and apply your ideas to conditions as they exist, not as you
would like them to be."

A training executive, new to an old-line transportation
company, was talking to the head of the engineering department about supervisory development. "We can make
some great improvements," asserted the training director.
"I've just been checking a program in human relations that
was conducted last year. It was simply terrible. The outline was old-hat and too general. Some of the outside
instructors were totally unqualified. Programs of this kind
are just time-wasters."

The engineering executive's face did a fast freeze. "You
really put your foot in it that time," observed an associate
later. "That program was Mr. X's brainchild, and he thinks
it accomplished wonders."

The Subordinate Position

If you are moving into a well-established department as
a key subordinate of its chief executive, your "getting
oriented" problems are narrower. Your boss probably hired
you and is available to give you guidance and counsel. You
may still encounter hostility from some associates, especially if you have been moved in over them. But their
resentment is human and passing. Your superior will give
you backing, and if you conduct yourself in a friendly and
diplomatic manner these initial obstacles will soon be
surmounted.

Nevertheless, you may yet run into difficulties. For example, if you are a specialist in some particular field of
management and your new boss has sold you on the idea

that he has an important and specific job for you to do,
don't be too surprised and too disappointed if executives
in other departments are not as enthusiastic as he is. Even
your own departmental colleagues may be a bit more
restrained in what they say about the need for your services than is your superior.

Many men are oversold on their new jobs. It can happen
to you. But don't hold that against the man who hired you.
He genuinely wanted you, and he thinks you are needed.
In most cases, he will give you full support in your assignment. Any failure on your part would reflect on his judgment. Also, you've got to be honest: If you have been
oversold, it's probably because you wanted to be. Wishful
thinking about greener pastures somewhere else has been
the downfall of many an executive career.

Said a market research man after a few months on a new
job: "I was shocked at the lack of resemblance between
my actual position and what the vice president in charge
of sales had said it would be. The company had never
done its own market research before. I soon discovered
that I was supposed to set up the staff and get the project
accomplished all by myself. My office was not as good as
my old office. Worst of all, my project was 'hot' only in the
opinion of my vice president. He couldn't get me the
budget he had promised. I was so disappointed I thought
about quitting. Then I remembered I was hired for a purpose, and it was up to me to work out the details. When I
buckled down and accepted things as they were, not as I
had hoped they would be, I began to make progress."

Some Pointers for the New Middle Manager

Here is some advice given by middle management executives on how to make progress during the first weeks
on your new assignment:

1. Be sure your attitude is right. Come prepared to do a job of work and give that job a real try.
2. Be sure you are receptive to new ideas and able to adjust to a new environment. You have learned many things from your past experience, but not all of them may be applicable in your present situation. Try to approach your duties from a fresh point of view. If you're inflexible, you only make trouble for yourself.
3. Avoid snap judgments. Before you decide anything about the methods you will adopt to accomplish your objectives, be sure you know that they apply. Don't size up people too quickly. You may be mistaken.
4. Don't commit yourself too early, especially about the details of how you will attain your objectives. You don't want to incur premature opposition.
5. Don't criticize your predecessor or the way he did things. You may antagonize his friends.
6. Don't go overboard in praising everything and everybody in your new company. Also, don't compare your old management unfavorably with your new one. You reflect on your own maturity by either practice. Your own associates can't help but note that despite the fact that you have left, your former company is still doing business at the old stand and getting along quite nicely, thank you.
7. Be ready to accept advice. Be sure that it's coming from the right source and that you are not being asked to pull somebody else's chestnuts out of the fire.
8. Don't be too disconcerted if some of your new associates are cold to both you and your program. You may be an unexpected and successful rival, a threat to their ambitions. Be natural. Then things will probably work out.

9. Don't look back regretfully to your old job. That's over. Forget it, and go all out to make a success of your new one.

10. Analyze carefully the power structure of your new organization. Try to discover quickly how your department fits into it. This will help determine the best approach to your job. However, make this study through observation, listening, and, occasionally, a few discreet questions. When an executive volunteers information about the politics or conflicts of interest between departments, don't accept it literally. Wait until what he says is confirmed from other sources before you allow his comments to influence you or your activities.

Some Problems of Middle Management Assignments

Here is the comment of a labor relations executive who joined an aircraft company. "Although an industrial relations job is usually considered staff, at my company I was assigned certain line responsibilities. We were in a cutback program, and my boss had been given authority to help decide who in our management organization was to stay and who was to go. Since I had a great deal of experience in organizational planning, my duties were to help make these decisions. It was uncomfortable for me to know I was new and permanent in a department and in a company which was releasing other men with five or even ten years' experience. It's a ticklish spot to be in if your new associates think of you as a hatchet man. Although I met no open hostility, I could feel the resentment of oldtimers whose jobs were in danger.

"As time went on, I built up considerable goodwill by trying to enhance the status of others. For example, when I first assumed my job I had to handle every grievance report—supervisors were afraid to accept this responsibility. Through my efforts we have increased their authority, and today I am concerned only with the last step of the procedure."

This executive went on to say that he had one thing working for him—his attitude. "I decided early in the game that my new company had been in operation a long time, so it couldn't have been doing everything wrong. I asked for help and got it. I realized I couldn't do much trouble shooting until I located the troubles, and to do this I needed assistance from people who knew where they were. Nevertheless, I think it took about four months before I was really accepted by the group."

The experience of a wage and salary administrator who shifted from a stable, conservative food corporation to a rapidly growing electronics company is another illustration of the orientation problems an executive faces when he moves into a high middle management job. This man's duties were entirely of a staff nature . . . but let him tell his story himself.

"At my new company, the authority of the man who handled wage and salary administration had not really extended to the executive level. He was concerned mostly with rank-and-file and supervisory compensation. My position carried the title "director of executive compensation," and I was brought in at a much higher level than my colleague. While he didn't report to me—this was to save his face—I realized that there was an overlap in our functions. So I tried to cultivate his friendship, discuss various problems with him, and ask his advice and help. Evidently he resented me very much. He made it a point never to visit my office unless I sent for him, and he had a habit of sending memos to the rest of the staff and excluding me. On one occasion he told me that I should avoid the treasurer of the company because the latter didn't like me. However, the treasurer needed my reports. I began to drop by his office to leave them, and occasionally, when I saw him sitting alone in the cafeteria, I would stop by his table to talk. We soon got on good terms. Later I learned the reason for his initial dislike of me: it was because my associate had told him I had designs on his job.

"My associate did his best to make my new job unpleasant, but since he was only a few years away from retirement I decided not to make an issue of it and run to my boss for help. Nor did I stoop to his tactics. I simply put our relationship on a strictly business basis and forgot about him. After seven or eight months he saw he was no longer getting under my skin, and things smoothed out. I still don't like the man, but we get along all right so far as business is concerned."

Pointing to another dilemma of the middle management executive, particularly when he is introducing a new service, this wage and salary man added: "I soon learned my company was not sophisticated in the administration of an executive compensation program. It is my job to sell line executives at the various plants on the merits of maintaining a systematic and unified program. During my first weeks I made a 'get acquainted' tour of all our plants. I discovered that insofar as executive compensation administration was concerned, each plant was in a different stage of development. This meant I had to revise my thinking radically. Instead of installing my program in a single operation as my boss told me would be quite practical, I learned I would have to sell it piece by piece. My objectives remained the same, but it took me three years instead of one to reach them."

A similar observation was made by another staff executive who had accepted a highly technical assignment with a plastics company. He said, "I spent a great deal of time during my first weeks on the job giving my boss a technical understanding of my field, which hitherto he had known only in a general way. He needed this information so he could speak authoritatively and knowledgeably to his own top management and to our board.

"My boss was very helpful. He accompanied me on a tour of our 20-odd plants and introduced me to their chief executives. This got me started on the right foot. If I learned anything during this period, it was the value of patience. The service I was offering was new to the company. I had to demonstrate that my assistance was needed. My boss told me that I couldn't expect to do this overnight."

Your Boss Can "Make or Break" Your Job

There is one more point to keep in mind if you accept a subordinate management position with another company. *It makes a difference who hires you.* A labor relations executive was persuaded by a consulting firm to take a job with another firm at plant level. He had been assured that he would have quick access to the vice president of industrial relations who had actually done the hiring. Things didn't work out that way. There were too many levels of management between him and the top, and he took orders from the plant manager—a stranger—not from the parent company's industrial relations executive. He finally resigned. "I didn't stand a chance of success," he said. "This plant hierarchy was too well established, and it liked things the way they were, not as the vice president of industrial relations said they would be. I should have done a better job of investigation before I took the position."

Another executive tells this story of his experience with a new company. "The first weeks went swimmingly," he said, "but matters changed as soon as I tried to get started on my job—executive development. The company was not really ready for the program my boss had told me it wanted. I soon saw that I would have to make another change. I made the mistake of trying to institute an executive development program in a company that was basically not prepared to accept it."

These examples underline the importance of finding out as early as possible exactly where your job stands in relation to the directing management. This is especially true if you accept a plant position and the top man who hired you is located at a far-away central headquarters.

A very capable industrial relations executive was named plant personnel director for a Midwestern company. He soon found that he had to clear every move he made with the vice president of industrial relations, whose office was in Chicago, more than 300 miles away. Worse than that, he had other "between him and his boss" executives whom he had to satisfy. "I spent my first month on the job finding out who my bosses were and what my authority was in relation to each of them."

Checklist for the Breaking-in Period

These experiences of executives with new assignments illustrate the types of problems that must be faced. How you personally fare will depend on the special circumstances that you encounter. However, here are some common-sense rules that may guide you comfortably through your first weeks in a new position.

1. Go easy in committing yourself to new friendships until you learn whether or not people's motives are self-serving and who among your new associates can really be helpful. Some of them will be more friendly than others. Accept their friendship pleasantly. But the volunteer friend who wants to take you under his wing may have other reasons than simply being a good Samaritan. Under his pleasant exterior he may also conceal an extremely sharp knife.

2. If you encounter hostility on the part of another executive or group of executives, find out why before you become too resentful. Maybe they think you constitute a threat to their best interests. Try to demonstrate that you are on the payroll to get a job done. Remain objective; don't get into needless arguments with associates simply to assert yourself. If you prove out, early resentments are likely to vanish.

3. Be careful not to align yourself with factions. It's better to stay "loose" as long as possible.

4. Avoid going to the mat over issues until you are reasonably sure you will be successful. Premature trials of strength never did anybody any good. However, don't pussyfoot. You were hired to do a job, so let it be known—not arrogantly or belligerently—that you intend to do it.

5. Be friendly with subordinates, but stay formal. It will take you a little while to discover who does what and how competent he is in doing it. Be very careful not to play favorites—especially if you have brought some of your own people with you.

6. Take part in company social activities when you are invited, even if you don't know your new associates too well. These activities give you an opportunity to get acquainted and find out more about the facts of company organization than you could during hours of conferences with everybody's guard up.

7. Don't accept the confidential information given to you by a new associate as literal and unprejudiced. Whenever possible, wait until what he says is confirmed from other sources.

8. Don't forget the friends who helped you get the job. Be sure you thank them for what they have done. You can do this unobtrusively by writing

them letters telling them how you are making out
on your new assignment and incidentally thank-
ing them for making it possible for you. Some of
these people may know your new boss better than
you do and may encourage him to be patient with
your progress.

9. Be compassionate with the associate or subordinate
who failed to get the job you were brought in to
do. His disappointment is human, and it may be
bitter. He deserves every opportunity to recover
his balance, and if you treat him in a natural manner he is likely to make this recovery more quickly.

10. Don't make changes until you have sufficient
knowledge of company personalities and practices
to be sure they are the right ones. Study the functions of each subordinate, and the ability of each
to perform those functions, before you make up
your mind.

11. Feed in new people slowly, and make sure present
job incumbents get every opportunity to demonstrate their abilities. If you do bring in new people,
try to fit them into your team on the same basis
as everybody else. Don't permit them to become
a layer of management separating you from your
staff. The executive who brings his own key assistants with him may discover that these assistants
are assuming authority he never expected them to
have and alienating him from the men and women
whose support he needs to accomplish his objectives.

CHAPTER III

HOW TO GET A GOOD GRIP
ON YOUR NEW JOB

WHEN YOU ACCEPT A NEW ASSIGNMENT, YOU CAN COUNT on that honeymoon period we've mentioned. How long it lasts depends on your job, the urgency of its problems—and you.

The ambitious executive wants to get started quickly. He seeks results and chafes during periods of inaction. However, the wise executive does not move into a situation until he is fully briefed on its complexities and has taken the time to consider exactly what he should do to reach his objectives. He weighs such factors as the nature of the assignment, the competence of his staff, and the interest—either pro or con—that the executives in other departments may have in his program.

It has been said that the honeymoon of a newly hired manager lasts until the day that his activities clash with the interests or projects of some other department. When this happens, it is up to the new man to prove his mettle. That is why premature decisions are unwise. You need a full evaluation of all the available facts to back your judgment before you make a decision. You also need a knowledge of the personalities involved. At the same time, you can't wait too long. Management expects you to get going. "We fired him," said the vice president of a certain company about one of its dismissed officers, "because all he

ever wanted to do was sit around and 'talk about things.'
I told him that we couldn't afford a staff philosopher."

Where's the Action?

"Where's the action?" is one question a fast-money
operator will immediately ask when he arrives at Las
Vegas. And it's a precept of a good combat general to
march his divisions toward the sound of gunfire. The competitive executive should take time to study his assignment
carefully and make proper plans on how to get it done,
but he should also remember that one fine day his company will expect him to show tangible results. When this
day comes, if all he can offer is excuses and promises about
tomorrow, he is in trouble.
    A vice president who had been brought in to create an
industrial relations department for a newly organized
holding company with plants in several industries was
abruptly summoned to the office of the president.
    "You have now been here for eight months. I gave you
authority to hire your own staff. Your department has already cost this company more than $200,000. What have
you done to justify your existence?" was the blunt question.
    The vice president could reply only that he was still in
the planning stage. "You are five months past your honeymoon," said the president, "so if you want your plans to
accomplish anything, they had better be good and you
had better put them into effect. Your department is overhead. Already I'm getting complaints from executives in
our plants that you and your 'experts' seem more like
tourists than people offering them a service. These men are
paying your freight, so you had better sell them on your
usefulness."
    "Competitive management likes executives who have an
instinct for the jugular," was a comment of the late Elliot

Janney, noted consultant. His expression is just another way of saying: "Get into the mainstream of the company's operations as quickly as possible. Management will give you time to adjust to your new environment. But don't delay!"

A hardbitten manufacturing vice president remarked, "The time to get things done is when you're new on the assignment. The company brought you in to make changes; psychologically, it's ready to accept them. If you procrastinate and delay because you're afraid to take risks or step on somebody's toes, resistance will harden and you will never get anywhere."

This executive continued, "The first weeks on a new job can be pretty harrowing and bewildering. But you may look back on them as ideally happy when the heat's turned on. Use your 'honeymoon' as a time to build a basis of solid relationships with your new associates. If they are sold on you and your competence, they will accept your ideas about their operations much more readily."

Picking Your Starting Point

"The main problem about getting started on a new assignment," said the corporate training director of a large Southern manufacturer, "is deciding what to do first. When I began this job, my 'in' box wasn't big enough to hold all the ideas for new projects that associates were sending me. In a panic I started riding off in all directions. Fortunately I got a grip on myself. I analyzed these suggestions, determined the relative importance of each, and developed my program accordingly. Here's my advice to a new manager. When you give one project precedence over another, you must be able to defend your decisions, especially to the man who thinks his recommendations are being sidetracked. The key to success on a new assign-

ment is your skill in keeping the initiative. If you let the
other fellow get the ball, you're on the defensive right
at the start. Seek suggestions and advice, but in the framework of your own program. You were brought in not only
to do a job but to have definite ideas on how to do it.
If you show weakness or indecisiveness in the field in
which you're supposed to be an expert, you won't win
much confidence in your overall executive competence."

"How did I get in the mainstream of my company's
activities?" an industrial relations vice president in a large
metropolitan newspaper reflected. "My first day on the
job my president told me that my primary project was to
start immediately on pension, group insurance, and fringe
benefit problems. Instead, I suggested that I start by making an analysis of what each executive in the first three
levels of management was doing. In writing the job descriptions of these top management functions, I got to
know the men who ran the company. I also learned as
much about their attitudes as I did about their responsibilities. When I completed my study I was able to come
up with some interesting and unknown facts about the
overlap of executive responsibilities. This enabled me to
present a concise program on how to improve overall
management efficiency and reduce cost.

"I enlisted the help of my chief subordinate, the personnel director, in the preparation of these job descriptions. We got to know each other very well and learned
how to work together. At the conclusion of the project,
the personnel director was given the job of writing similar
job descriptions for everyone else in the management
organization.

"Here are some of the things we learned: Some executives were overloaded with details; a number of executives
were duplicating each other's efforts. There were also tremendous gaps in the organization where nobody had the
specific authority to handle definite managerial responsi-

bilities. For example, purchasing! This was being done by three or four people who maintained little or no liaison with each other. Such a method was costly and inefficient but easily corrected. When I made my report to the president and his top staff, he quickly revised his thinking on what I should do. 'Your next project,' he told me, 'is to help us organize the responsibilities of this management for the most effective performance possible.'

"I didn't get around to straightening out pension, insurance, and fringe benefit problems until I had been on the job for more than a year. By that time I was so familiar with the company and its difficulties that I knew exactly what to recommend."

A. C. Thornton, vice president of industrial relations at Yale & Towne, gives similar advice to a top industrial relations executive beginning a new assignment. "You can't judge the best approach to your job until you are a good judge of your associates. There is no better way of learning a new assignment than by learning the responsibility and authority of your colleagues. The more quickly a man understands the duties of the people who run the organization, the more quickly he can match his activities with theirs."

"The first assignment of any new executive," said a management organization expert at an automobile company, "should be to analyze the functions of his department. When I accepted this job I made such a study. I learned that certain department heads did not understand exactly whom they reported to; in several cases a man might even have five or six bosses. A new executive can begin a job in no better way than by defining the functions of the persons who are responsible to him and by straightening out lines of authority. You have to know who does what and by what authority before you can move effectively into your own job. Good management means good communication and cooperation."

This is also the advice of a seasoned management man who added, "I came to my present job through a consulting firm which had done a great deal of work for the company. I spent my first weeks holding talks with my subordinates and with associates in other departments. I wanted to learn precisely what the consulting firm had recommended as to the reorganization of the company, and how these recommendations tied in with my responsibilities. I had this information from the president, but it was necessary for me to learn whether other members of his management team had the same understanding. It's surprising how differently various people interpret the same set of recommendations, particularly as these apply to them and their responsibilities.

"It's well never to get your associates upset over plans and programs until you know the score yourself. As a result of my discussions, I learned that the immediate problem I had to solve concerned personnel. Change was needed in one key spot in order to make a $75 million operation turn from red to black ink. It was plain that this losing operation required a capable production manager. We had such a man at our Midwestern plant, so we moved him east, and terminated the Eastern manager. Within a year the new man had straightened out the basic production problems of the Eastern plant and made it profitable. What happened to the Western plant? The assistant to the man we transferred was ready for promotion."

As a newcomer you have definite advantages. For one thing, you may question the customary. Too often, old-timers have grown so used to doing things a certain way that they shrug their shoulders and assume nothing can be done to improve matters. Because you have a fresh point of view, you may be able to spot breakdowns or inefficiencies in many company activities that your colleagues accept as normal. This will enable you to make specific suggestions for improvement. Your initial recommendations may be preliminary or temporary. But at least they plug a hole and give you time to make permanent improvements.

"Don't be afraid to rediscover the wheel," said the top officer of a transportation company. "When I took this job, some of my ideas seemed so elementary and so obvious that I thought past managements must have considered and rejected them for reasons that were obscure to me. I learned that this had not been the case. The real reason nobody had taken the steps I proposed was because my predecessors had thought, 'We can never get away with it.' I believed that at least my ideas were worth a try. You would be surprised at how many things you can actually accomplish if you can persuade people to go ahead and do things that they have always thought were impossible."

Clarify Your Objectives

A prime requisite of getting a new assignment under quick control is your ability to zero in on your target. It is important to evaluate and classify projects in order of importance.

"When I accepted a position as head of a national manufacturers' organization," said its executive vice president, "I saw that there were three crying needs: more members, more money, and a complete reorganization of the financial department. However, money came first. We therefore introduced a new line of services which brought in cash and expanded certain activities which returned a revenue. The increased cash flow enabled us to extend our full line of services and add new members to the staff. This increased our efficiency. It also enabled us to 'sell' more new members. When these things had been done, we were able to modernize the methods of our financial department. Had we attempted this modernization first, we would have gone out of business."

It is usually a mistake to sacrifice sound, long-term goals for fast and flashy dramatics. Sometimes, however, the spectacular is desirable to show that you are putting an organization in motion. But even if your assignment calls for quick and revolutionary initial action, don't mistake eye-catching improvisations for solid achievement. Plan for the long haul, and never confuse shadow for substance. Even if circumstances force you to move more rapidly than you had originally intended, be sure the gaps in your program are quickly caulked with substantial follow-up. If you don't you may find yourself in the position of a general whose tanks have scored a sensational break-through in the enemy's lines but who can't win the battle because he lacks the infantry to exploit his gains.

The vice president of public and industrial relations for a well-known national company explained this technique when he said, "To be successful my department had to get going fast. During my first year on the job we went all out to publicize our programs, many of which were still on the planning board. Top management was amazed and pleased with the attention we were getting from the press, from stockholders, and from other companies. I knew all this was simply window dressing. However, behind our public relations façade my staff was rapidly and quietly building sound and workable programs. We built the roof first but made sure that everything we put under the roof would stand the test of hard examination. During that period, I made it a point to follow up on every detail of every program. I couldn't afford mistakes."

How to Build Your Own Management Team

In addition to deciding the relative importance of the various assignments that compromise your overall responsibility, there is also the essential and simultaneous task of selecting your team. Here are some of the questions which must be answered during your first weeks in office: Which of my subordinates are competent? Whom can I trust? Do the people already in key jobs have the ability to do them the way I want them done?

How you go about selecting and building your own organization depends on the particular problems that you must solve. The authority of your job is also a factor. It is usually wise to have a frank discussion with the man who will be your chief subordinate. Explain your objectives to him and win his support. It is not necessary to describe your plan of action in detail. Proceed with caution in talking about the specific implementation of your program until you are absolutely sure of yourself. There is no need to bind your movements early in the game by outlining a detailed approach to your goals, when later on you may find it advantageous to reverse your field in order to reach them. However, you can and should outline general objectives to your key subordinate. It is also common sense to listen to his advice about the difficulties you will meet. His evaluation of personnel may be useful. You don't have to accept it literally until you know how reliable it is. But at least it will give you the feel of your organization.

The vice president in charge of sales at a machine tool company said, "I had several long talks with my sales manager during my first weeks on the job. His appraisals of the key people in my department were accurate and helpful. When you take a new job, you can almost depend upon it that there will be a troublemaker. My sales manager identified a man who would give me this kind of headache. I was careful not to accept his criticism at its face value, but I soon found he was right.

"The best thing to do," continued this executive, "is to show from the start that you will put up with no nonsense, that you expect the cooperation of subordinates, and that such cooperation will be recognized and rewarded. Make it equally clear that failure to adjust to a new administration has only one result—dismissal."

A competitive executive knows that change is resented by many people, and this kind of resentment is marked by failure to cooperate. Such failure is either passive or open. If it is open, you have no difficulty in identifying the source and taking remedial steps. The person who makes no bones about resisting your authority can be handled by frank confrontation. You hold the cards; he has to adapt himself to your methods and approaches or get out. But if opposition is covert, if a subordinate gives you lip service but secretly attempts to frustrate your general design—perhaps even by literal compliance with your instructions—you may find his resistance harder to meet. You have to get across to everyone concerned that you are calling the signals, and that employees who fail to follow them because they either didn't hear or don't agree with them have no place on your team.

If you are charged with ultimate accountability for the success of an operation, you cannot permit your authority to be challenged. You should listen to the suggestions and ideas of subordinates, but when you make a decision you must make it absolutely clear to everybody that you expect—in fact, require—that they do what is necessary to make it work. There is no better time to demonstrate this than during your first weeks on a new job. Your people will know that while you are open-minded, receptive to good ideas, and tolerant, you also demand results.

The Leader Sets the Pace

Responsibility is a hard taskmaster. It requires long, hard hours of work. One management consultant observed, "You may have gotten your job through personality or contacts, or because of your skill on the golf course. But unless you can prove yourself by performance, you will soon lose it. Friendships have a habit of cooling off fast when a manager discovers the friend to whom he gave a job can't produce."

The best way to win the respect of subordinates is to show by your own performance that you are willing to spend the time and effort to make your department a success. Management usually gives its key people plenty of leeway in deciding how to handle their jobs. But don't abuse this freedom.

The president of a highly successful paper company remarked, "We have no policy on vacation or days off for top executives. They can take as much time away from their jobs as they wish. I have only two criteria for judging the performance of a key man. Is his department successful? Does it contribute to our profit picture? If the answers are 'no,' we get another man."

You are given certain responsibilities, and management expects you to produce. Management also expects you to spend as much time on the job as your assignment demands—and so do subordinates.

The vice president of industrial relations at a heavy machinery company said, "Too many times a man is simply unable to cross over from routine minor manager to full-fledged executive. When the whistle blows at quitting time, this kind of executive beats the clerks and workers out of the plant. If a person is unwilling to accept the hard hours that go with authority, he should be satisfied to remain in an undemanding job."

When you are new on an assignment is the time to show that you are eager to do what is necessary to make a success of it. You set the pace. Your subordinates will respond more quickly to your leadership if it is fast and decisive. If they see that you know where you're going and that you don't intend to shilly-shally getting there, your enthusiasm will be reflected in their work. A quick starting pace creates an invigorating work climate. It also enables you to see who among your subordinates can keep up.

Here is what a successful industrial relations man said about the importance of getting off to a fast start. "If you move forward swiftly and surely, you will soon learn which of your subordinates can make your team. I don't advocate motion simply for the sake of motion. You have got to identify goals. But you can't spend forever getting set for the take-off. If you do, you will certainly lose the built-in initiative that is yours simply because you are new on the job and management expects great things of you."

What to Do About Staff Deadwood

Dismissal is a tool that you can't use every time you seek to eliminate problems caused by an inefficient executive. Sometimes a subordinate is a fixture in the company and dynamite won't blast him out. Perhaps he is only a few years from retirement, perhaps he has done outstanding work in the past and sickness or some other problem has robbed him of his ability, perhaps he is the president's son-in-law. Whatever the reason, he is your headache and you're stuck with him. When this happens, you have to accept the realities of the situation and do your best to get as much from his performance as possible.

No executive can expect to have a staff of worldbeaters. All-star teams are hard to come by and are seldom inherited. The experienced manager learns to get the best from the tools he has, including personnel. Still, you will find that if you immediately crack down on people who aren't producing and terminate them, downgrade them, or snap them into line by some other method, the morale in your department will move up. Your subordinates know

who is doing his job, who is goldbricking. They respect
a boss who can spot the goldbricker.

These suggestions offered by experienced executives
may help you cut deadwood from your staff.

1. If you have inherited a nonproducer in his early
   60's, start right away to persuade him of the advantages of early retirement. If he is a troublemaker, don't hesitate to call the shots. Retire him
   as soon as possible.
2. Study the characters and habits of your subordinates. The man with the sloppy approach, the
   man who is harassed and overburdened by detail,
   the man who shows an unwillingness to adjust to
   change, the man who constantly takes time off to
   go shopping for his wife or who figures out ways
   to take advantage of policy (for example, extend-
   ing his vacation by fitting it in with a long weekend), the man who thinks like a nonexempt employee about his job and the time he should devote
   to it—these are usually not the kind of people you
   can trust with responsibility.
3. Don't tolerate open defiance. If a man can't work
   your way after you have looked at his way and decided it's not good, he has no place on your team.
   Don't let sympathy or an unwillingness to take on
   an unpleasant duty deter you. Get rid of him—
   quick.
4. Keep records. The old notebook technique is still
   pretty good. You don't want to rely on second-
   hand information in judging subordinates. Make
   your own evaluation. Don't make mistakes by moving too soon and on inadequate information. Never
   is morale destroyed so fast as when deserving people get a fast shuffle from a new boss.
5. Recognize achievement early and don't stint on
   praise. But be sure you are recognizing the right

person. If you give credit for a good job to a fast
talker when it really belongs to somebody else,
you do more harm than good.
6. Get salaries into line as quickly as possible. The
real producers in your department may not be
earning the salaries they deserve while other people are hauling home the big pay checks. It will
probably take at least six months before you can
begin to make these adjustments, but your long-
range plans should include straightening out all
pay inequities.

How to Spot Minus Factors in Subordinates

One executive has supplied a list of minus factors that
are helpful to a new executive in evaluating inherited
subordinates. He says: "In judging people, here are some
storm signals that you should carefully consider in building your management group."
1. Watch out for the fellow who is pigheaded and
insists on doing the job the old way. He is stubborn
and probably limited in his outlook. Unless there
is a good reason for his rigidity (there is always a
possibility that he is right and you are wrong),
slot him for routine work or help him find a job
somewhere else.
2. Be discerning about subordinates; judge them on
performance, not articulateness. Many a man
makes a good first impression because he "talks
a good game." If you have such a subordinate, be
sure to check early to see if his gift of performance
measures up to his gift of gab.
3. Don't be tolerant of bad personal habits. They are
usually a sign of immaturity and bad judgment.
At one plant the personnel director could not learn
to behave like a manager. In spite of warnings,

he dressed like a beatnik and insisted on sitting on everybody's desk. His abilities did not outweigh his drawbacks, and he had to go.

4. Crack down hard on the subordinate who spreads rumors or talks too much about the inadequacies of your new approach. Make it plain to your people that you are willing to listen to their criticisms and hear their advice, but let them know that the man who is not loyal won't last.

5. Don't wink at the subordinate who allows certain of his responsibilities to slide. Give him adequate directions and then insist that he do his whole job, not just the parts of it he likes. Such a person is likely to blame somebody else or have a thousand and one excuses when you find that some aspects of his job are left undone. If he is incapable of carrying out all of his responsibilities, relieve him of those parts of his job which he can't do and give them to someone who can.

6. Beware of the man who is too much of a homebody, who always has a personal reason for not undertaking an away-from-home assignment. Every subordinate should know that with you the job comes first. If a position requires a man to travel from time to time, or to put in extra hours during emergencies, it is up to him to meet his obligations. If he wants the prestige and pay of a managerial position, he must accept its responsibilities.

7. Be wary of the glory seeker, the fellow who grabs credit for a job that is really a team undertaking. Unless he can correct his faults, he is resented by his associates and will never acquire real leadership ability.

8. Discount and eliminate the subordinate who depends on pull or position instead of solid work to advance his career.

9. Keep an eye on the subordinate who complains about the inadequacy of his salary and cites his children's education or the high cost of living as reasons why he should have more money. Evidently he doesn't relate his job to his compensation. Also, he is a bad morale factor because he is probably talking to everybody else.

10. Don't play along with the man who is always complaining that he is not getting the breaks. Undoubtedly he is telling everybody within earshot that you're prejudiced against him. It's also likely that he is not doing his own job properly. He hasn't got time. He's too busy complaining.

How to Spot Plus Factors in Subordinates

It's never wise to judge a subordinate purely on negative factors. A seasoned executive tries to acquire the balanced outlook. One company president listed the following qualities among those he uses to identify subordinates who could help him carry the ball of company responsibility. He says:

1. The man who will help you most is the one who is willing to give your way the old college try. He listens to your proposals and makes suggestions that will sharpen them. You can learn much from what he has to say. But when you have made your decisions, he does his best to gear his actions to accomplish what you want.

2. A man who is willing to work the necessary hours to get a job done gets a plus sign by his name. Try not to be unreasonable, but key subordinates have as much cause to make the company successful as you do. Their time is the company's time. They should see it that way—if they want management responsibility and pay.

3. The people who will push forward on a project whether you are there or not deserve recognition and advancement. Too many executives let things slide when the boss isn't around. If you have a man who moves on his own initiative, he is a jewel and should be treated as one.

4. Mark the man for advancement who gets your directions right the first time. Such a subordinate asks intelligent questions to fill out your instructions when you have been vague or too brief.

When you are new on an assignment, you may be fooled by some people. But if you're perceptive and know your own job, you will quickly correct such mistakes. In most cases, you will be able to spot the "comers"—and the "goers." When you have finally decided that a subordinate doesn't measure up—and never will—let him go. The longer you keep him around, the more difficult it will be for you to give him the pink slip.

Follow-up, Communication, and Performance

Follow-up is always important, but never so much so as during the first phase of a new assignment. You are working with new people, and you can't take anything for granted. In the early part of your career with a company mistakes hurt. It's urgent for you to check on delegated assignments. Follow-up is the best way to become acquainted with your people and evaluate their abilities. When you believe you are on top of your job and have finally decided how much supervision each of your subordinates needs, you can relax.

Keeping yourself informed is a necessity, but don't ignore any aspect of communication. Progress reports to both your subordinates and your superiors are essential. All of the standard methods of communicating are useful

—written reports, memos, private discussions with key individuals, and conferences.

The conference is particularly helpful in keeping your staff informed. "During my first three months on the job," said a successful utility company executive, "I held a conference with my key staff members three times a week. I made certain these conferences were short and sweet—10 to 15 minutes. A new man can make a serious mistake if he has 'conferencitis.' If you keep your people tied up in meetings they never get any work done—and, besides, you bore them to death."

Another executive warns, "If you hold staff conferences, keep them small. A meeting attended by 15 or 20 people is seldom useful as a planning device. It is too likely to be draggy. Call big meetings when you want to explain plans, procedures, or policies and are prepared to answer questions about them."

Discussions with your subordinates will give you a keen insight into their attitudes and abilities, but there is no better or quicker way to gauge a man's ability than to observe him in action, especially on a major project.

"When I took charge of the industrial relations department at my company," said a top labor relations man, "my staff was in despair. The company had been losing money, and its labor relations were in bad shape. For years the unions had run all over management; the industrial relations people could get nothing done. I was a member of a new management team that came prepared to act. We made mistakes, but there was a change in management atmosphere. Executives in every department soon saw that the new officers expected to put the company in the black and correct its problems. A new spirit developed, and people buckled down and went to work."

Slow motion at the beginning kills spirit. An executive attending a management seminar had this observation on the danger of procrastination: "We hired a bright young man to set up an organizational planning department. He chose to spend all his time drawing up formal organizational charts. They looked pretty, but somehow his assignment never got completed. We finally told him that unless he produced something we would simply have to conclude he was not the man for the job."

Keep the Support of Superiors

The support of superiors is an absolute essential to a new man. If he dissipates it through delay in getting started, through lack of direction, or for any other reason, his tenure in office will no doubt be brief.

"When I took a job with an insurance company," said one labor relations executive, "I learned that in the past the management had been a pushover for the union. The company had many customers which were unions and didn't want to lose their business. I had stipulated that I must have management support to clean up the mess. During the first months I bent every effort toward selling my program to the officers and keeping it sold. When the union struck us because of our stiffening attitude, I had management support. We went through a long work stoppage but were successful in getting the contract we wanted. Now things are much better. I have the respect of my superiors, and the union has a new respect for the company. P.S.: We didn't lose any union business either."

A more unhappy example is that of an extremely bright and personable young management development man who lost out at a company which had offered him a promising career. Here is what his boss said: "His ideas were good, and the programs he outlined were excellent. But he didn't take the trouble to sell them and keep them sold. Whenever he met resistance, he wilted. His attitude was, 'Why should I bother to persuade executives to accept my plans if they are too stupid to see how good they are?' We let him go with the explanation that if a man can't develop his own executive abilities, he won't be much good in helping other people to develop theirs."

Your Relationship with Consultants

Management consultants—headhunters, if you like—are responsible for placing many competent executives in new assignments. Perhaps you got your new job through one. If so, he may be helpful to you now. He probably knows the company and can give you background information on your new associates. Since the company is—or has been—his client, and he recommended you for the job, he is anxious for you to make good.

His study of the company and its problems led him to suggest that someone with your special talents be brought in to help straighten out specific difficulties. Therefore, if you detect an inefficiency in an operation for which you are responsible, and you are as yet not quite certain how to remedy it, it may be a good idea to have a talk with him. His views may clarify your thinking and enable you to make specific recommendations. If special executive talent is needed to cope with the situation, he may be able to help you find the right man.

However, you—not the consultant—were brought in to do the job. Don't rely on him as a crutch. Your company doesn't want to pay your salary and also pick up his bill, especially since it believed that your joining the organization would solve the problems he detected. The experienced executive knows when to cut the string. Nor does he rely too much or too long on a consultant to help him with internal company problems.

One finance executive failed in a new position for exactly that reason. He had been placed by a consultant, and he couldn't cut loose from his mentor. Every time he had a problem, including resistance to his program by other associates, he hotfooted it to the consultant's office with anguished cries for help. "You didn't tell me about this. Things aren't working out the way you said they would," was his constant complaint.

Finally the consultant told him, "I have no power to help you. My firm diagnosed the problems of the company and recommended you as the man to help straighten things out. You had better buckle down and do things on your own. We didn't promise that we would be your nursemaid. And you are proving we made a mistake in judgment."

Some Tips on Taking the Initial Steps

To sum up:

1. You were willing to take a chance in accepting your new assignment; so be willing to take chances in getting things done. Just don't gamble foolishly. When you take a chance, try to line things up so your project has every reasonable chance of success.

2. Don't hesitate to innovate. Your fresh point of view is among your most valuable assets.

3. Since the company is psychologically prepared to accept your recommendations, you will probably be able to accomplish more than your predecessor, particularly if you win veteran executives to your side. They may see you as the man who can introduce the changes they have long recommended but couldn't get accepted in the past.

4. Keep an eye on costs and establish your reputation as a man who is careful with the company's money. Cost-saving applications introduced during your early days on the job make you look good.

5. Check your progress. Be sure you have developed some method to see how your program is advanc-

ing and how to measure where you stand. If you are in a line or sales operation, you can check the books. If you're in a staff position, progress may not be so easy to measure. Still, you are wise to develop a system of indicators and guidelines to show you how you are doing.

CHAPTER IV

HOW TO KNOW HOW
YOU ARE DOING

N<small>O ONE WHO EVER KNEW HIM THOUGHT HE WAS WEAK</small> or hesitant in dealing with any problem that confronted the company. But he was too smart to think that by being tough for the sake of toughness you became a good executive. His strength was dedicated to the fulfillment of his assignment. He understood that the use of power for selfish advantage or to demonstrate that he had power was the straight road to personal failure and that it would have disastrous effects on the company. These broad principles guided his career. It was a privilege to have worked for him."

These words were spoken by the executive vice president of a large manufacturing company about his chief officer, who had died of a heart attack at the height of his career. The executive continued, "I doubt if it ever crossed his mind to wonder what people thought of him, or how well he was doing his job."

A wonderful tribute to a successful industrialist! But you can be sure that there were moments when he wondered what his subordinates thought of him; wondered whether or not he was measuring up to his duties. Had he totally lacked the ability of self-analysis, had the qualities of reflectiveness and introspection been completely missing from his make-up, he would not have been the leader that his subordinate pictured him. True, his years of accomplishment had given him confidence and poise. He could cover up his inner feelings and present to the world a calmly assured demeanor. But underneath he was intensely human.

His wife remarked, "My husband was a perfectionist. But perfectionism came hard. Decisions affecting the future of his company and the livelihood of so many people worried him. When some serious problem had to be solved, he couldn't sleep. Not many people knew this side of him, for he was always careful to conceal his anxieties. But I think it was worry and concern about his responsibilities that killed him."

The Fear of Failure

Psychologists say that fear of failure and fear of sickness are the twin terrors of the successful man. These two fears are closely linked. Obviously a man who is driving hard to reach specific objectives fears a protracted illness, since this might prevent him from accomplishing his design. Furthermore, there are few people who are so self-assured that they are not concerned with appraising their progress or do not wonder whether they have succeeded in winning the support of colleagues.

Naturally you have considered the consequence of failure, for it is always a possibility. However, if you keep your fears and uncertainties in perspective, they can be quite helpful. They become spurs that encourage you to use the best of your abilities. "On a new job it is always wise to 'run a little bit scared,'" is the advice of most experienced executives. The trick is not to let others sense your uncertainties.

When Herman Hickman was football coach at Yale, he remarked, "I like to win enough games to keep the alumni sullen but not mutinous." This wry comment on the trials

and tribulations of a football coach underscores a basic
principle of executive leadership. You must make sufficient
progress to keep your superiors satisfied. How you go
about getting your job under control, handling people, and
evaluating your progress depends on the nature of your
job, the extent of your responsibilities, and your own personality and methods.

What It Takes to Be a Leader

There are no set rules of leadership. Winston Churchill
was a brilliant conversationalist. He was imaginative,
warm, and outgoing. He liked a brandy and enjoyed a
good cigar. On the other hand, Field Marshall Montgom-
ery was laconic. He was a teetotaler, and he abhorred to-
bacco. Both were extremely successful in persuading people that they knew what they were doing and that their
decisions were the right ones.

The question of your personal popularity is not para-
mount when it comes to deciding your competence as a
leader. However, you must secure the respect and confidence of people, particularly subordinates. One top executive puts it like this: "Employees must believe you are fair,
that you expect a job from them. If you are doing the job
yourself they will live up to your expectations." Another
management man observed, "The boss isn't running for
'Queen of the May,' but he'll probably get a lot more done
if people don't dislike him thoroughly." Finally, an industrial relations director commented, "You don't have to be
really liked to be a good executive. But you're in hot water
if your subordinates think you are an enemy. If the people
who work for you despise you, they can cause you plenty
of trouble."

There are many types of successful leaders: the quiet
boss who gets the job done in spite of a soft manner and a
considerate approach; the hard-driving authoritarian who

exudes self-confidence and is constantly prodding his people to push forward; in between, every gradation of leadership. Henry Ford built an automobile empire, but even his greatest admirer, Charles Sorenson, admitted that Mr. Ford was never particularly well liked by his associates. Evidently this did not bother him in the least. On the other hand Harvey Firestone, another industrial pioneer, was warmly regarded by other executives both in and out of his company.

There is no single prescription for leadership, but there are several qualities all good leaders share. They are at their best when the chips are down. They are not afraid to make decisions—even if they worry about them. They have a single-mindedness of purpose in the pursuit of their objectives. They know how to persuade others to accept their decisions and turn the decisions into realities.

The Shadow and the Substance

Today the term "executive" has become a sort of status symbol in our industrialized society, a title that is as highly prized and as eagerly sought after as was a patent of hereditary knighthood in Great Britain during the 19th century. However, the executive career is an uncertain one. Few people have the opportunity, as did the heroes of Horatio Alger, to begin at the bottom and work their way to the top. Executives shift jobs constantly, sometimes for a better opportunity, sometimes because they fear a cutback, sometimes because they find their services are no longer required. The man who mistakes the shadows of an industrial career (expense accounts; country clubs; travel; stock options) for the substance (a desire for accomplishment; long, hard hours; the willingness to make unpleasant decisions and take reasonable risks) is likely to find himself on the beach in his late 40's or early 50's with the opportunity of a second chance exceedingly remote.

A successful company president summed it up: "An incompetent or semi-competent manager can get along all right so long as things go well. He may even work his way into a position of authority. Such an exposure to responsibility illuminates his shortcomings and weaknesses. His performance is constantly being appraised by everyone. If he falters or fails, his treatment is ruthless. That is why it is so important for a man to evaluate himself. Many an executive looks like a million dollars when he enjoys the protection of a strong boss. But when he succeeds to his boss's job, he simply can't stand the gaff and folds like an accordion. A person who accepts responsibility should make absolutely sure he wants it and is capable of bearing it. The man who is dazzled by a big title and its perquisites because he yearns for the surface trimmings of success is in for a hard time. Unless he is very lucky, he is likely to lose everything."

Your experience in management should have taught you how to evaluate yourself realistically. (If it hasn't, there is no advice, however good, that will be of help.) You realize, therefore, that in your new job you must win organizational respect. Whether or not people like you socially doesn't make too much difference. However, most management men agree that the executive who is fair and square and treats his associates and subordinates with respect is the one who survives when the heat is on—provided he has the abilities and courage that are demanded by the job.

Vanishing Resentments Are Proof of Progress

Practically every management appointment of any consequence means heartbreak to someone. You can be almost certain that there are persons in your company, even in your own department, who may be a little bit resentful. They think they can do your job. They think they deserved the chance to prove it. In fact, they may even have been counting heavily on the opportunity that went to you.

This kind of resentment can be hard to handle. But it is also useful. As it wears away, it becomes a sort of progress report on your own accomplishments. "I knew I was set," said a sales vice president, "when my top assistant walked in and told me, 'That was one helluva presentation you made on our new sales campaign. Everybody's talking about our program. I'm really proud to be a member of this department.' I knew this man had hoped to get my job. During my first weeks in office he had been correct but formal. Here he was genuinely pleased about my success and unconsciously translating it in terms of team accomplishment."

Another executive recounts a similar experience. "I received a promotion that a colleague thought he deserved. I had never finished college and my colleague had. Friends told me, 'Watch out for that fellow. He's constantly complaining about how an uneducated man like you can get a promotion when he can't. He has a graduate degree in your field.' Six months later I overheard a conversation between my erstwhile critic and another person who had asked where I had earned my degree. 'My boss didn't finish college,' was the rejoinder, 'but he has proved to me he knows his stuff and knows it better than nearly any college graduate you can name.' I realized that I had been right to keep quiet, treat this man like everybody else, and ignore his resentment. I relied on my performance to prove to him that I knew how to run the department."

If you are perceptive, you will be able to detect resentment, and in most cases you will be rewarded by seeing it evaporate as you take charge. However, there are a few hard cases. The best thing to do is to treat such people naturally and act in a perfectly normal manner. If they believe that they are getting under your skin, matters won't be helped. Furthermore, if you lean over backward to gain their goodwill, you will probably be unsuccessful. Overtures of this kind are likely to be construed as a sign of weakness. You may even lose the support of colleagues who are disposed to like you. Such actions indicate that you are unsure of yourself.

Said an experienced manufacturing man, "There were one or two people who resented my appointment as vice president, but I paid no attention. I soon discovered that my new associates were my best defenders. A vice president of another division told a certain backbiter who had made a belittling remark about my work, 'I don't agree with you at all. I think he is doing a splendid job. What's more, you would help yourself if you stopped griping over little things and gave him support. Your attitude is not doing you a bit of good around the company.' When this conversation was reported to me, I was sure I was making progress."

Of course, there may be isolated instances when it is necessary to have a showdown with an unreasonable and carping critic, especially if he is a subordinate or an associate. It may clear the air. When such a confrontation is necessary, don't dodge it. Use judgment and be sure of your facts. Also be as objective as possible, and keep away from personalities.

A training director said, "I walked into the office of a man in my department who had been most unreasonable in his attitude toward me. Bluntly I told him, 'I'm fully aware that my appointment to this job was a disappointment to you. I don't blame you. I also know that you have done everything in your power to interfere with my operations. You don't have to like me. You are free to disagree with my methods. But if in the future you usurp functions that come under my control, attempt to countermand my orders, or do anything else that prevents me from carrying out my assignment, we are going to have a showdown. I might as well learn now as ever whether our boss wants me to do the job he hired me to do. This time I'm talking to you—next time both of us will see him!' For many months we were cool to each other, but he never bothered me again. I soon found that by standing up to this man, I won greater respect from other people in my department. After the incident, everyone was much friendlier."

Results Count but Attitude Is an Index

Good performance, good manners, administrative knowhow are the hallmarks of executive success. If you combine these three ingredients of sound management, there will eventually be tangible evidence of progress. What evidence? That depends on the nature of your assignment, but here are some examples: greater efficiency of operation, lower costs, higher volume of sales, better morale among employees, tighter controls, improved industrial relations climate.

It will take time for this evidence to accumulate. However, there are early straws in the wind which will tell you whether or not your associates believe you are headed in the right direction. These won't be obvious. But when an associate drops by your office to ask advice about some problem that is bothering him, you can usually be sure that he thinks your advice is worth having. Also, if your suggestions are listened to respectfully by associates or superiors at conferences, you have another indication that you are fitting into the management team.

After the "honeymoon," you will be able to detect whether or not you are winning acceptance for your programs, your ideas, and yourself. Here are some signs:

1. How often does your superior call you in to discuss departmental problems? If you are left in your office to look out the window, maybe he has not been too impressed with your competence.

2. When you ask to see your boss to report on activities, is he readily accessible, or does he put you off? And, when you do finally see him, does he say, "I'm very busy this morning, so let's get to the point quickly"?

3. Are the assignments you are receiving increasingly complex and challenging? Are you given more and more freedom in carrying them out? If your superior is constantly checking on the details of your work and is overly cautious in allowing you to represent the department with other executives, you probably have not won his confidence.

4. What about associates? Do they frequently invite you to join them for lunch? Do they discuss company problems with you on a give-and-take basis? When you wish to talk things over with them, are they easy to see?

5. Are your suggestions or recommendations usually well accepted by other departments—or do they resist your efforts or seek to delay your plans?

Any one of these signs in itself may not be conclusive. Nor should you worry too much if all your recommendations are not enthusiastically seized upon. You will meet some resistance. Nobody's progress toward success is a steady march of triumph.

"I was hurt during my first six months with the company because I seldom, if ever, got in to see the president," said a manufacturing executive. "I thought he was giving me the brush. After I had been around a while, I found that this was his way of operating. So long as you were doing all right, he left you alone. But when I ran into real problems I learned that he was on top of his job, knew all about mine, and gave me every help in solving my difficulties."

The attitudes of subordinates can be a useful means of appraising job progress. Among the significant signs that you should observe are stepped-up morale, enthusiasm for assignments, greater team pride. How do these attitudes show themselves? Here are a few ways: Subordinates make worthwhile suggestions to improve your original plans. They volunteer to accept additional assignments. On their own initiative, they push forward projects which they know you consider important.

One executive, comparatively new on his job, explained, "You can literally feel the forward push of your department when you have won the confidence of people. Their actions tell you better than words that they have sized you up, believe that you are giving them the right sort of leadership, and have accepted you as boss. When my staff completed a report two weeks earlier than I had expected, with the explanation that the men in the department had realized how important it was, I knew I was getting ahead."

An engineer said, "I realized that I had truly become a part of our organization when a pipe in the plant burst about three o'clock one morning. Normal procedure would have been to ask maintenance for a plumber. My supervisors realized that this would delay production, so they fixed the pipe themselves. I would never have known about it except for my secretary. She said, 'You've certainly got the night-trick supervisors on your side. They want you to make a good record. You're the first boss who ever showed up on their trick two or three times a week to give them a chance to tell you about their problems and to have you explain your plans.'"

You don't have to be a psychologist to know that the human factor is very important to your success. That is why it is a basic principle of leadership to know as much about your people as possible. In the process you will also learn a great deal about how you are getting along. Subordinates are quick to know when their superior is on the spot. They are tuned in on the company grapevine, and if they judge you and decide that you don't measure up, their opinion will quickly get around the company.

Stay in Character and Be the Boss

Knowing your subordinates does not mean buttering them up. Flattery or trying to be one of the boys gets you nowhere. The main thing is to stay in character. The gregarious boss who encourages give-and-take exchanges with his people and is on a first-name basis with everybody from the president to the office boy may do a splendid job. But the fact that he is a friendly and outgoing person isn't the reason. The real reason is he knows his job. Subordinates realize that he expects their best at all times and that he doesn't hesitate to crack down when necessary. They may swap jokes and stories with him, but they don't take liberties. Nor do they mistake his attitude as an open invitation to "take-it-easy street."

On the other hand there is nothing sadder than to observe the naturally aloof, self-contained person trying to be something different because he thinks that is the way to win goodwill. "Call me Tom," one executive vice president encouraged all his key people, and reluctantly they did. But it was always forced. Behind his back they called him "the archbishop" or "the prime minister," because they realized that his invitation to an intimacy that did not really exist was totally false. This particular executive was capable. But he was also formal in his manner, lacking in a sense of humor, and inept at small talk. His attempts to step out of character and get down to what he thought was the level of his subordinates only made them feel uncomfortable. The "one big happy family" approach isn't too successful unless the members of the family are enthusiastic about their jobs and take pride in getting them done. In this case, the "family" feeling is incidental.

Your principal goal is to carry out your assignment efficiently. You have probably read that managers who are "people centered" accomplish more than those who are "job centered." Notwithstanding the pompous sociological phraseology, these terms are essentially correct if you understand their exact meanings. In your job as manager you must be "job centered" through people. You can't succeed in your assignment unless you are totally "job centered." However, you must keep in mind that the specifics of your position will be undertaken by subordinates. It is your responsibility to outline goals clearly and explain carefully how each person is accountable for doing his part to achieve them. Subordinate motivation is founded on excellence of leadership. And subordinate cooperation, not mere compliance with orders, is a significant sign of job progress.

The techniques you use to develop a competitive work team depend on the methods you have learned from experience are best for you. However, successful executives know it is not their responsibility to mollycoddle mature men and women, plead for their help, or overlook their faults in the hope of being considered a "nice guy." Executives who believe that they are some sort of den mother catering to the whims or special desires of employees are probably doomed to failure.

The Need for Communication

The willingness to communicate is usually strong evidence of good leadership. The fact that you are willing to talk things over gives you a keen insight into the problems of subordinates. They get a clearer understanding of your problems and consequently are better able to help you solve them.

The industrial relations vice president of a New England company said, "There is no better formula for winning fast cooperation than by letting your people know early in the game what your plans are—both short- and long-range. No one likes to work in the dark. People who don't know their boss's goals don't know whether what they are doing is important or not. As soon as I took my job, I made it a point to meet often with everyone who reported to me and to emphasize repeatedly how important each of their jobs was.

"The feedback was tremendously helpful. For example, I learned the faults of our incentive program under which run-away rates were hurting the company's competitiveness. We took prompt corrective measures and saved the company a great deal of money. I made it a point to let top management know which of my subordinates had been most helpful in this revision of the system."

Another top executive observed, "Upward communication is extremely important to a new man who wants to know how he is doing. The more intimately you know your people, the more precisely you can delegate. After I had been on this job a few weeks, I learned that the wife of one of my key men had multiple sclerosis. I realized that this would hamper his travel schedule. I made some shifts in staff duties and gave him equally important assignments that would keep him in the office most of the time. I had a frank talk with my subordinate and explained my reasons. He was delighted. I learned that he had been afraid to mention his home problem to my predecessor because he thought it might hurt his chances of promotion."

Good two-way communication also provides you with detailed knowledge of what's going on in your department. The alert manager knows the exact status of each project for which he is responsible. Employees respect a superior who has a complete comprehension of what they as individuals are doing, how they are progressing, what difficulties they are encountering. It is sometimes hard for a new boss to get such knowledge. Until he has it, he can't come to grips with his full responsibilities. Furthermore, he can hardly hope to convince subordinates that he considers their work important unless he knows precisely the duties which have been entrusted to each of them.

"The best way to get to know your people is to know their jobs," advises an experienced plant superintendent. "You can't represent your department or protect its integrity unless you are aware of the details of all its functions. This involves knowing all about the men in charge of these functions."

Employees quickly sense when a boss is floating around at the top with no real grasp of what either he or they are supposed to be doing. When people get this feeling, they lose their sense of direction. They also lose confidence, and this shows up in loss of morale.

According to one executive, the best way for a new man to evaluate his progress is to determine how confident he is in giving orders. If he is moving ahead, he becomes more and more certain every day that his decisions are the right ones; that he knows what to do and how to do it. The man who is floundering knows he is in trouble, and it shows up in his leadership. He may be able to cover up for a while, but it won't take long for everybody to know he's in trouble too.

Hard Proof of Job Progress

The collective experience of many executives provides sound standards by which you can measure your progress on a new job. Briefly, these standards may be summarized as follows:

1. Tangible evidence is the best proof that you are making the grade. If you are in manufacturing and production figures have gone up, efficiency is greater, and there has been an improvement in quality of goods or services, you can reasonably assume that you are passing the test of performance. If you are in sales, after you have been in your position a reasonable time the company's order books tell at least part of the story of how

well you are doing. If you are in industrial relations and turnover drops, union relations improve,
or better training increases employee efficiency,
you can be reasonably sure that you are doing all
right.

2. Intangible evidence is more difficult to gauge, but
it supplies important pointers on job progress.
Better coordination of company or departmental
affairs, less bickering and greater cooperation between departments, improved morale of subordinates, a greater understanding of mutuality of interests between executives—all are indications that
your leadership is bringing results.

A Checklist of Executive Performance

In writing this chapter to explain how new managers
appraise their personal performance, how they build competitive departments and staffs that give support and loyalty to company objectives, literally hundreds of executives were consulted. The following is a checklist of do's
and don'ts that has been compiled from their combined
experiences.

1. Don't worry too much if one or two people in your
department—or in the company—resent your appointment, at least at first. If you do your job
properly, this feeling will disappear. But be wary
of the man who can't overcome his resentment. If
he has power, he may work openly to discredit you.
If this occurs, don't run away from a showdown. If
you have a balky subordinate—and have given him
every chance to come around—get rid of him. You
can't tolerate disloyalty.

2. Don't pay too much attention to company gossip.
But listen and take the advice of mature associates
who can help you learn who is doing what and

where the important problems are that you are expected to help solve.

3. Check the resentment barometer periodically. Subordinates who were at first aloof and correct but
are now warm and enthusiastic, associates who
were politely noncommittal but are now cordially
friendly—these are sure signs that you are making
progress.

4. Go slow in socializing. Let associates make the first
moves. But don't be too stand-offish, or you will get
the reputation of being a snob.

5. Be sure you are able to do any job that you accept.
If an assignment is beyond your power to accomplish, ask for help. Don't try to bluff it through.

6. Give credit to your top producers. They are the
ones who make your reputation. Use performance
as your criterion, and never get hooked by a fast
line. Subordinates resent it when good men are
bypassed for promotion and credit is given to people who don't deserve it.

7. Don't get bogged down in detail. As boss, you have
to know where the trees are, but you must also be
able to see the forest.

8. Watch for the big signposts of job progress—first,
acceptance of programs; then, policy recommendations that have been installed and are now paying
off.

9. Don't be fooled by flattery. Much of it may be self-
serving.

10. Don't play favorites. Lean over backward to be
fair.

11. Don't hesitate to reorganize your department and
revise assignments when necessary even though
you may bruise a few feelings in doing so. Your
job is to get efficiency in operations. Furthermore,
judicious reorganization may expose some hard-

headed opponents of your program and, at the same time, indicate the men who are adaptable and willing to meet new challenges.

12. Don't rely on written appraisals of subordinates, particularly if they were made by your predecessor. At best, such appraisals are only indicators. Judge your people for yourself, and base your judgment on personal knowledge.

13. Be willing to give praise when it is due. The best boss gets the best people to work for him.

14. Never become complacent or take praise at its face value. Everybody flatters a winner, but this kind of backslapping can become backbiting the minute you falter.

15. Be willing to work longer and harder than any person you supervise. A superior who loads down his staff and then heads for the nearest golf course is never very popular, even if he says he is going there to talk business.

16. Tell your subordinates how they are doing. Make it informal—at lunch or incidentally during a discussion of departmental plans or problems.

17. Watch the attitudes of associates. Are your ideas solicited? Do colleagues ask for your opinions at conferences and listen to you when you give them? If you are frequently interrupted when you start to give your point of view, it may be that your associates don't think what you have to say is worth hearing.

18. Make a periodic check of your own job progress by trying to see how well you know the details of your operation: who does what and why.

19. Don't alter your manner or try to buy the goodwill of critics by playing politics. Be yourself.

20. Don't mistake being well liked for doing a good job. Always evaluate your performance by accom-

plishment. When associates like your programs and recommendations, you are better off than if they simply like you.

21. Keep things in perspective. While a poor performance during your first six months may break you, a good performance won't necessarily make you. It simply gets you off to a good start. Your eventual success depends on your stamina over the long haul.

22. Never ask how you are doing. This shows you are uncertain. The frank appraisal by superiors of your programs, recommendations, and suggestions is the true tip-off. If your proposals are chalking up a rate of acceptance, you are in high gear and will stay that way so long as they work.

CHAPTER V

THE SOCIAL SWIM

MAN IS A SOCIAL CREATURE; WOMAN, EVEN MORE SO. THE income from your job provides you with the money to live in a pleasant home, give your wife and family the things they need and enjoy, pursue your hobbies, and entertain your friends. But your business life is a part of your existence that your wife and family cannot share except peripherally, any more than you can take a major part in their personal daytime activities.

You and your wife probably have many friends in common. Very likely you share many interesting activities. But just as you are the captain of your ship in business life, your wife is in charge of social matters.

The Social Overlap

True, in the modern environment an executive's business and social life are not things totally apart. There is an overlap. Undoubtedly you will develop pleasant relationships with associates at the company, and they will inevitably lead to social relationships. Furthermore, you and your wife will be expected to take part in some company social functions. How often and what kind depends on the philosophy of the company, its location, and your own desires. If the company you work for is in a small town, social life may center around the organization. This may be a help or a handicap depending on you.

"We stepped into a ready-made social life," said a manufacturing vice president who moved to a small town in Illinois. "My wife and I love it." On the other hand, a top management man who moved to a rural community in Pennsylvania resigned after a year or so. "My wife couldn't take it. We were expected to be a part of all sorts of community affairs and to entertain back and forth. We like to stay by ourselves and to have a few close friends outside of business. There was too much gossip and backbiting. People knew too much about each other, and we couldn't stand this kind of environment, so we left."

It would be presumptuous for any writer to advise a mature executive on how to conduct his private life or to give him tips on how to be a social success and be accepted by his community. What you do is up to you. Maybe you and your wife are recluses; you don't care in the least about social activities except on your own terms. If you are reasonably pleasant at the office and do your job, such an attitude will make little difference.

A highly successful finance executive told his president flatly that while he would come to a meeting of top management at a resort hotel which wives were expected to attend, his wife would not be there. "My wife is not on the payroll, and she doesn't like this kind of affair. Since business will be conducted at this meeting, it's my job to be present. However, if the meeting were purely social, I wouldn't come either."

The president was surprised, but he respected his subordinate's decision. Did it hurt? Three years later this finance vice president became president of the company. He knew his job; that was all he needed.

On the other hand, many an executive career has been speeded forward through the efforts of a wife who is a gracious hostess and gets along well with the wives of other company officers. If you are gregarious and your wife is too, there is no reason on earth why this should not be an asset to your career.

A deft hand socially wins many opportunities; but, generally speaking, opportunity is all it wins. You still have to implement opportunity with quality performance to get what you want. If you rely exclusively on the social route to achieve your ambitions, you will probably get lost on a detour. "It's not what you know but who you are that counts" is a cynicism that has ruined many people who believed in it. The man who has good contacts gets better breaks than the man who doesn't, but he still has to have job ability to make his initial advantage pay off. The fellow who marries the boss's daughter generally gets ahead. But if you examine the pre-marriage careers of men who have done so, you will probably find that most of them won the right to meet the boss's daughter by their outstanding competence and ability. Even in a family-owned company, the best the not-so-bright nephew of the president can expect is a high-sounding title, a good salary, and no real responsibility—that is, if the family expects the company to stay in business.

Your wife will plan a campaign aimed at becoming part of the community. She knows all about the Welcome Wagon, the Newcomer's Club, and various other organizations that help recent arrivals enter into a community's life. In most cases, she will choose the church you attend (unless you have strong religious views), see to the children's schools, and be the first to know your new neighbors.

Naturally she will seek your advice on many of these matters. She knows your likes and dislikes. The wife of a recently transferred executive remarked, "I went to several churches before I made a decision on which to join—and I went alone. My husband thinks most ministers are so liberal and so political that he wants to answer them from the floor. It's hard enough to get him to go to church at all, so I try to find one where the preacher and the congregation are not totally in conflict with his ideas."

The Question of Churchgoing

Two or three generations ago choosing a church—or a school—was relatively simple. If you were a Presbyterian, you went to the Presbyterian church—and unless you were extremely well off and had a private-school tradition in your family, your children went to the nearest public school.

At present this is often not the case. Executives move from community to community so that the feeling of having roots in a tradition or a religion may largely be gone. "When I was in Ohio, we went to the Baptist church; when we were transferred to California, we attended a Methodist church; but since moving to New Jersey, we have become Episcopalians," remarked the wife of a frequently uprooted executive. When asked why, she replied, "We go to the church where most of our friends go and where we like the minister."

This point of view, so frequently heard today, indicates the changing nature of churchgoing in the contemporary community. Whether for better or worse, theology is no longer much of an issue. A sociologically oriented society places its reliance on good works instead of adherence to formal creeds. Members of parishes normally appear to be little concerned with the attitudes and beliefs of their clergy, as evidenced by the wide differences of opinion on the issues of the day between the Federal Council of Churches and the people of its member congregations. For the executive moving to a new community, participation or nonparticipation in church activities is a matter of individual inclination and has little to do with his social acceptance—unless the community is old-fashioned and, probably, rural. Many people now go to church because they think it's the right thing to do, and they send their children to Sunday School because they think this also is proper. But when 50 executives were interviewed recently on how they went about selecting a church when they moved to a different location, most of them seemed surprised that the question was even asked. A large minority said they were "in and out" attenders of religious services, and a majority thought it did not make any difference socially whether they went to church or not.

"You meet some people at church whom you would like to know socially," said one man, "and if you are using a church as a means of getting acquainted, it probably works for some people. But me? I go to church with my family because I was brought up that way. The people in my congregation who are friends of mine would have been friends of mine anyway. I met them all somewhere else— at clubs, at cocktail parties."

The attitude of a community toward church attendance depends on the character of the community itself. People in a sophisticated high-income suburb will have totally different views on this matter from, say, the inhabitants of a small rural town where the church may also be the center of social life. Therefore, if your new assignment lands you in a small rural community and you take no part in church activities, you may be somewhat conspicuous and some people may even criticize you. However, people are increasingly tolerant today. So long as you are a good citizen and don't belittle the beliefs of others, you can probably do pretty much what you like about going to church no matter where you are—and it will have little effect on your social life.

The Problem of Schools

Social considerations aside, the question of schools also is very important. If you move to a small town, you probably have no choice—the public schools are all that are available, and to them your children go unless they are old enough and you can afford to send them away to preparatory school. However, if you are moving to a metropolitan area, the quality of the schools should be carefully considered. Unless you live in a suburban community where schools still provide quality education, you may find it necessary to educate your children privately, and this is expensive and getting more so. An executive moving from Indiana to New York City exclaimed, "It costs me $2,000 a year to send my two grammar school children to classes. Of course, I send them to private schools. We prefer to live in the city, and I wouldn't dream of sending my kids to a New York public school."

This attitude is the rule rather than the exception. New York City, for example, maintains an extensive private school system to satisfy the educational requirements of middle- and upper-income people who do not care to expose their children to the sociological and political problems that beset the city's public schools. And, when you remember that it may cost as much as $1,500 a year to send a 12-year-old child to a private school as a day student, education becomes a serious financial factor. The wise executive has investigated the school situation thoroughly before he accepts a job in another locality because he knows that the cost of education may be a large item in his budget. Even a sizable increase in salary may not be sufficient inducement to take a job in a metropolitan area if you have school-age children who must be sent to private schools.

"I refused a transfer to New York," said a middle management engineer. "I simply couldn't afford the opportunity. Even though the salary meant a $2,000-a-year increase to me, when I considered the cost of education my budget couldn't take it. I could have picked a suburb where public schools are still excellent, but that would have meant commuting, and commuting is costly."

Clubs and Their Use

Clubs are a pleasant part of any community's social life, and they are useful in your business. "I do a great deal of business at my club," remarked a successful Philadelphia executive. "The atmosphere is relaxed, and you can have a leisurely lunch with good service. Nobody is hurrying you to vacate your table. If you haven't finished your discussions when lunch is over, you can always continue your talk in the club library. People are often flattered when I take them to my club instead of to a restaurant. They like the environment. This means they are inclined to be more receptive to my ideas."

There is no doubt about it; clubs—aside from the social opportunity they offer—have a certain prestige value. The friends you make there, especially if you are living in a smaller town, will help to make you feel at home. However, while many clubs in big cities do have a certain amount of prestige, they are rather like private hotels. Men use them for business, and it is doubtful if the friends you make there will enlarge your circle of social acquaintances appreciably. If you live in Westchester, north of New York City, and meet a friend at your Manhattan club who lives in the Oranges in New Jersey, it is not very likely that your families will see much of each other. The same thing is true of any large metropolitan area where your social life will be largely confined to the suburb in which you live.

Country clubs, unlike men's clubs in the city, do provide you with a variety of pleasant social opportunities—golf, dances, bridge parties for your wife, receptions, and the like. Moreover, you will meet many of your business associates there.

A vice president of a large New York company remarked, "Aside from the pleasure of the program my country club provides, I find it very useful in business. Every time I am faced with contract negotiations, I meet with the vice president of another large company which deals with the same union, and we talk things over during a round of golf. We have both benefited from these discussions. There are no interruptions, and we are relaxed."

If you are interested in the life that clubs provide, there is no doubt that they will add to the social enjoyment of your new community. But the question is, how do you join? The initiative is not yours. Your company can help, particularly in the matter of men's clubs. Very probably some of your new associates will bring up the matter and suggest that you join them for lunch at their clubs. This is probably a preliminary to inviting you to join if you show interest. Also, if you formerly belonged to a club which has reciprocal arrangements with a club in your new community, you may be able to manage a transfer. However, on this matter, don't move precipitately. The club to which you are transferring may not be anywhere near as good as your former club, and if your first move to a new community is to join a "poor" club, it may not help you much socially.

What you do about your club life depends on the type of community to which you are moving. If it is tradition-bound and set in its ways, it probably does not put out the welcome mat for newcomers, particularly in the matter of social clubs. It may take your wife five or six years to join that garden club she thinks is so nice. Some clubs are practically closed to everyone who doesn't have the right social credentials and sponsorship. This is particularly true along the Eastern seaboard. The likelihood of a stranger becoming a member of an ancient and exclusive dance club in any of the large cities of the East Coast is remote unless he can acquire powerful sponsorship. Even with such backing, it will take time and patience before his membership application is accepted. The children and relatives of present members usually get preference.

However, clubs of this kind are for the relative few, and you can still have a full social life at the clubs that do welcome you. Associates at your company will be helpful in putting you up for business and golf clubs—if you show that you are the type of person whose company they will enjoy. So far as women's clubs are concerned, they are a matter that your wife will have to manage. Naturally, wives of associates at your company can be helpful, and if you have moved to a relatively small town they will probably make it a point to assist your wife by inviting her to join their activities.

However, there is one common-sense point to keep in mind. No matter how anxious you are to join a club, don't make the first move. You don't want to get the reputation of a "pusher." A millionaire industrialist who moved to a seaboard city had set his heart on joining the yacht club. He was evidently under the impression that the club was very exclusive, for he approached the president and offered to rebuild the docks if admitted to membership. The club president was furious that this man had attempted to buy his way in, and as a result the millionaire was never invited to join. Actually, the club wasn't exclusive at all. The dues were only $17 a year, and if the industrialist had simply allowed his name to be put up in the normal manner, he would have encountered no difficulty in joining.

You may be able to discuss the problem of clubs frankly with your boss if you have a close relationship with him. If not, an associate with whom you have struck up a friendship may be able to give you good advice. However, the wise thing to do is to let this aspect of your social life develop normally. If you are perceptive, you will soon sense the atmosphere of your new community. If you are pleasant, and your wife and family fit in, you will have no serious problems. In the natural course of events, you will be "in."

It Depends on the Community

If you move to a smaller town, the social transition will probably be easy. You and your family are newcomers and have something fresh to add to people's social lives. If the town to which your new job takes you is the kind whose social activities center around the company, your social life will be ready-made.

However, if you are moving to a metropolitan suburb, fresh from a small town, you may find your first months hard. This is particularly true if your wife is not accustomed to big-city living and yearns for the warmth and informality of the close-knit community where she once lived, where everybody knows everybody else and everybody knows just where he stands. The suburbs are filled with people just like you. Nearly all of them are from somewhere else, and many of them don't expect to be around very long anyway. In this transient environment, the wives of many executives become unhappy, and there is really nothing you can do about it, except be patient, until the adjustment is made. It probably will be. Human beings are remarkably resilient and learn how to adjust to new conditions with comparative ease.

Guide to Fitting In

Although an executive is fairly free to lead the kind of private life he and his family enjoy, there are certain basic social realities that still apply and always have. The following suggestions—compiled from interviews with more than a hundred executives who have been transferred or otherwise moved—may be helpful to you in accomplishing such a transition:

1. *Be adaptable*. Things are different in your new home town. You are a newcomer, and this may be something of a comedown. You have to start from scratch and make new friends. However, if you are natural and pleasant you will soon find compatible people who enjoy the same things you do and who will add much to your social life, just as you do to theirs.

2. *Don't be a character unless you are absolutely certain you can get away with it*. The maverick with ability is in an enviable position. He can take an unpopular stand on issues, ignore traditions that everyone else accepts—and get away with it. But the maverick has usually demonstrated that he has unusual competence. His associates have decided they will tolerate in him habits and opinions that they won't accept from others. The young writer who complained that he couldn't understand why he wasn't famous because he drank like Edgar Allen Poe, used laudanum like Samuel Taylor Coleridge, chased women like Lord Byron, and held unpopular political opinions like Percy Bysshe Shelley overlooked a very important fundamental. It wasn't the faults of these men that made them great. It was their genius. You don't have to be a conformist to get along, but you do have to use a measure of tact. There is no need to be contentious, argumentative, or controversial.

3. *Crusade on your own time*. If you or your wife have pet projects or causes that you wish to advance, don't let them interfere with business. You are paid to do a job, and you will get along better if you devote full time to it.

4. *Don't take the obvious initiative in social matters.* You will soon develop cordial social relationships with associates, and these relationships will lead to social invitations. But don't make the first move. You are the newcomer. Return invitations when you think this is desirable. You are open to criticism if you move into a new community and hold "get-acquainted open houses."

5. *Use judgment in your social relations with superiors.* Just because the boss invited you and your wife to dinner doesn't mean that you are supposed to ask him for a quick return engagement. Perhaps his reason for asking you is merely to extend a welcome, and he is not necessarily anxious to establish a "home and home" social arrangement with you. It is always good judgment not to be presumptuous in social matters with company superiors—at least until you get to know them well enough to decide how close a relationship they want.

6. *Maintain formal social relationships with subordinates.* With subordinates a pleasant-but-aloof relationship is usually best. Your invitations to them are by their very nature almost command performances. On the other hand, if you are overly friendly with one or two people on your staff outside of office hours, other staff members may resent it. When you do invite subordinates for a social evening, stay away from business talk unless it is of a very trivial nature. Also, be impartial in such invitations, and make sure to include all those who ought to be there whether you like them or not.

7. *Develop as many social relationships outside of business as possible.* If certain associates at the company are a part of your social life because they are also a part of the community's society, well and good. But if your social activities are centered

around people you know at the office, your private
life becomes inbred. Moreover, its very narrowness
may lead to complications. It will be more relaxing
and pleasant if you know a variety of people whose
interests and conversation are different from the
talk you hear at the office.

8. *Don't encourage your wife to discuss business.* The
wise wife knows all about her husband's business,
but she doesn't discuss it with people from the
office. Wives who give their opinions on company
actions or policies, who complain that their husbands are not getting proper recognition, who are
quick to criticize their associates, usually harm the
husbands' careers.

9. *When visiting business associates, take your cue
from the hostess.* Social affairs that are attended
exclusively by company executives and their wives
are semi-business. Follow the conversational leads
offered; if your hostess is trying to make the occasion light and pleasant by means of small talk,
don't introduce serious topics. Above all, stay away
from business. And remind your wife that conversation about the doings of children, difficulties at
the laundromat, and the high cost of shopping is
fairly dull and should be kept to a minimum, especially among relative strangers.

10. *Study the atmosphere of your community.* If you
live in or near a big city, your social life can be just
about what you make it. Unless you get 'way out
of line, nobody knows or cares what you do and
whom you see away from the office. However, if
you are living in a smaller community people
watch you more closely, and it's common sense to
observe the accepted forms.

11. *Don't be a name dropper.* You don't impress strangers by telling them how important you were in

your old home town or how many important people you know. If you are really important and count distinguished persons as your friends, the word will get around. It's better coming from somebody else.

12. *Your wife can be a help.* The careers of many men have been given a boost because their wives have been tactful, gracious hostesses who knew how to create a pleasant and cordial home atmosphere. If your wife is the kind of person who knows how to talk to other people and appear interested in what they say (whether she is or not), she can be invaluable to you in entertaining business associates and their families. However, it's wise to size up situations. If you take your wife to a conference, and she is the only woman there, you may put a strain on her and everyone else. Bring your wife to business affairs if it's appropriate; leave her home when it's not. If in doubt—why take chances? Go stag!

13. *Be yourself.* You can ignore every suggestion that appears in the foregoing list and still get along amazingly well. These suggestions are not hard and fast rules anyway; they are only pointers about pitfalls you may want to avoid. If you are natural, genuine, and sincere, you won't need any advice on the social do's and don'ts of getting along in a new community. You can rely on your own good background and social instincts to guide you. The man who needs a book of rules on proper social behavior is probably beyond help anyway. The main thing is to let the new community and your new associates at the company invite you to take part in their social activities. If you are pleasant and show that you are receptive to such an invitation, you can be sure it will be extended.

CHAPTER VI

SOME FINAL WORDS—
ESPECIALLY FOR TRANSFERRED
EXECUTIVES

THE MAN WHO CHANGES COMPANIES WHEN HE CHANGES
jobs has greater problems than does the transferred executive. He has abruptly ended one career and started another. His environmental change is almost total—a new
employer, a new community, new associates, a new home,
and, probably, a broader and more demanding assignment.

An Easier Time

The transferred executive usually has an easier time of
it. He is working for the same management and has a
greater feeling of career continuity. He has already met, or
at least talked to or corresponded with, many of the people
with whom he will work at the new location. Probably in
the past he has even visited the plant or office which is
now his headquarters. There is less feeling of strangeness,
and his familiarity with conditions will remove much of
the strain from the period of getting adjusted.

Here is what an executive who came to Princeton, New
Jersey, from one of his company's West Coast operations
said: "Fitting into my new job was a piece of cake. I already knew the majority of the top men at our Princeton

research installation and they knew me. My wife and I even knew many of their families, so we weren't absolute strangers when we came to town. My transfer was in the nature of a promotion. I knew precisely the job I was expected to do, my reputation at the company was long established, and I didn't have to prove myself. About the only real problem we had was to find a place to live and get our children started in school."

Another executive who had been promoted to a bigger job at a different unit of his company remarked, "I was relaxed about the move. I knew my boss and had worked with him before. I also knew some of the management personnel. They gave me the facts on schooling, housing, and transportation. Also, I understood company policy on transfers, so I knew exactly how much financial help I could expect from the company. If you worry about moving, you shouldn't work for my firm. I have been transferred before and will be again. If the company stops transferring me, it probably means management thinks I have reached my level. I don't want that to happen until I get to company headquarters."

In his comments on transfers, this executive made two telling points. The first: He was limited in his ability to negotiate with the company on moving expenses. An executive whom a company is trying to persuade to accept a position with its management has greater bargaining leverage. But you lose this "bonus baby" status if you are already on the payroll. The majority of managements observe definite policies about paying the moving expenses of transferred employees. In unusual situations, they may make exceptions to these rules and grant special concessions.

The second point regarding transfers is also worth examining. If you work for a large multi-unit company, you may be expected to accept transfers as part of your training program. The man who wants to stay put had better work for a company which is located in one place. Some managements think that the man who refuses a promotion if it means a move somewhere else is also saying, "I'm satisfied where I am and don't want further promotions."

A highly qualified scientist reflected, "My company offered me a better job and more money in Chicago. I like it where I am, so I turned the chance down. I know that I probably won't be asked again. But I'm good at my job, and I'm satisfied. However, had I been a line executive and rejected such a transfer, I probably wouldn't have lasted long with this company. It expects line managers to be more ambitious than us scientists."

Must I Accept?

Although a man may not actually put his job in jeopardy if he rejects a transfer, usually he doesn't help his career. Most competitive companies consider that their executives should go where the work takes them.

The president of one large firm remarked, "An ambitious man knows that his own convenience is secondary to the company's. Like a good soldier, he goes where he is needed. Managerial responsibility is not all beer and skittles. The fellow who won't go to the job because he doesn't like the local conditions isn't the kind of man to whom we want to give responsibility. He has shown he will accept it only on his own terms."

"You must make the best of the situation, however you find it," said a production man from a company in the electrical industry. "I have been transferred six times, and I'm not through yet. But each time I got a transfer, I was given a promotion. My company wants its executives to know all of its operations, particularly if they are being groomed for top jobs. Before I'm through, I hope to land at headquarters in New York. But you don't start at the top. You must prove you deserve to be there."

"I was transferred 23 times," explained a railroad executive, "before I became a company vice president and settled down at company headquarters. I was 50 before I found a permanent home. My wife and I knew that so long as I kept getting transferred to bigger jobs, I was still on the way up. We didn't mind too much. In a way we liked it. We have friends throughout the East who live in places where I once worked."

This philosophical attitude about impermanency is almost essential if you expect to make your career with a large national company. But some men, particularly if they feel pressure from their families, simply can't take it.

"When I heard I was to be transferred," said a capable engineer, "I took the job of vice president of manufacturing at a small local company. My boss thought I was crazy because I was giving up my future. But we liked our home, and the job I got suited me. I was tired of the rat race, and I didn't want to be always on the move."

The Friends You Leave Behind

The man on his way up in a company has problems that do not face the executive who has taken a bigger job with another employer. "It's difficult to be working with a fellow one day and be his boss the next," is a nutshell summary of the dilemma.

When you get a promotion, both your business and your social relationships with former associates change. The minute you are named boss, yesterday's associate automatically becomes a subordinate. You and he are no longer on the same level. Many companies, particularly large ones, minimize this problem when possible and practical by transferring a promoted executive somewhere else. But even a transfer does not fully solve the problem. As you move higher and higher in your company, it is inevitable that you will have men working for you who "knew you when." You can retain their friendship and keep their loyalty. But don't fool yourself. When you rise to a higher position and a higher income level, with rare exceptions these former associates no longer play a vital part in your business or social life. They belong to the past, and they know it just as well as you do.

A minor department head at a transportation company was talking about one of the key vice presidents: "We went to college together, and we are still good friends. Once or twice a year we go fishing together. But that's about all. We like each other very much, but we simply don't have the same kind of lives. What would I be doing out with the high brass? And he has to be with them."

A railroad department manager once told a young trainee, "Ten years from now, you will probably be my boss. So here's some advice. Your associates will never resent your being promoted over them so long as you deserve it. After you have been a man's boss for a few months, he practically forgets that you and he ever worked at the same level. As time goes on, he even takes pride in having known you when you didn't amount to much. But in a big company you never know when you may be working for the man who today is working for you. Be fair to everyone. Respect people as individuals. Then you will never have any trouble being boss so long as you have what a boss needs—competence and courage to do the job."

What should your relationship be with an old friend or associate who is now your subordinate? What attitude should you maintain? Here are some suggestions from executives who were interviewed on this question.

1. *Be natural.* Don't pretend a relationship that no longer exists. If you have a close personal friend who is now a subordinate, and your families have a standing social relationship, keep it up if you wish. But use judgment. Don't try to push such a

friend into the social activities of executives at your
level. It may be embarrassing to them and it certainly will be to your friend.

2. *Don't patronize.* Apart from the personal disappointment of the colleague who didn't get the job
you received, former associates are probably sincere in congratulating you on your promotion.
They will do a good job for you. But don't go
"big shot." Prove to them that you have earned
promotion by competence.

3. *Don't high-hat.* There is nothing people like better
than to see a stuffed shirt deflated. Don't upstage
former associates. You depend on their loyalty
and cooperation for your success.

4. *Don't play favorites.* If you have a friend who is
also a subordinate, don't give him special breaks.
His advancement should depend on his ability,
just like everyone else's.

5. *Don't be one of the boys.* You are in charge, and
subordinates expect you to be boss. Don't try to
make it easy for them to accept you in your new
role by pretending everything is as it was before
except that you have a new title. Assume responsibility with dignity and assurance.

6. *Don't let a subordinate presume.* The fact that
someone knew you before you were boss doesn't
give him any special privileges—even if he is an
old friend. In such a situation make it clear to the
subordinate that while you hope that your friendship will continue—outside of office hours—he has
no favored status at the company and on any
matter relating to company business. Actually he
is not such a good friend if he tries to take advantage of your friendship.

7. *Be discreet.* In your new responsibility you have
access to more information about the company.

Don't try to prove your importance by blabbing facts about company business, particularly to subordinates, to prove you are "in the know."

8. *Rely on performance.* Your right to be entrusted with management responsibility depends on your competence. Seek advice, and use it if it is good. But don't dodge decisions. You are paid to make them.

The Challenge Is the Reward

The president of one of America's large companies retired in his early 60's. His career had been a saga of success. He was rich, and his family life had always been happy. Seemingly, he was in the best of health. Yet in a depressed moment he put a bullet through his head. "Why wait for the inevitable?" was the cryptic note found on his dresser.

Some men live for competition. They seek challenge and, like Alexander, become despondent if they have no more worlds to conquer. Money, provided they have enough of it, is secondary. They are achievers; once the need for achievement is over, they have tremendous difficulty in adjusting to leisure.

In 1960 Professor David C. McClelland, a psychologist at Harvard University, published a book called *The Achieving Society.* It is based on years of research conducted by Dr. McClelland and his staff. Two of its points may be summarized as follows:

1. Achievement motivation is a key factor in national growth, since a rise in achievement motivation generally precedes an accelerated growth period and a fall in achievement motivation generally precedes a decelerated period.

2. Individuals who are high in achievement motiva-

tion are more often found in business or industrial spheres and are usually much more successful than individuals lower in achievement motivation. In short, a high achievement motivation is an important qualification for a successful business career.

You can be low in achievement motivation and still have a happy and full life—but not as an executive. Dr. McClelland observes that many scientists, research people, and, in fact, college professors don't score in achievement motivation and that they are not interested in a competitive business life. This is no reflection on them. They have sized themselves up and prefer to work with intangibles.

However, the temperamentally noncompetitive executive is in for an ulcer-ridden existence. The very nature of such an executive's job demands that he get results. Some big companies can support large numbers of staff consultants—psychologists, economists, anthropologists, or sociologists—and profit from their advice. But these people are overhead, and the funds to support their activities come from the work of executives who manage the business. While their contributions may be great, they are dependent on the executive who takes the risk and keeps things going. This is the way things are and always have been.

A Roman emperor—who rose to the purple even though he started life as a humble legionnaire—remarked to a friend, "Now that I rule the world, I can indulge myself with an attendant philosopher. I value his advice. But I still make the decisions."

Character and Pride

Only you know how genuinely competitive you are. The fact that you have accepted a new and bigger assignment indicates that you are ambitious and willing to take risks. However, the ingredients of your motivation for achievement are known only to you. If money, title, or the empty pride of prestige are your basic incentives, you are in for a rough ride. You may have worlds of ability, great technical knowledge, and high intelligence, but if the competitive element in your character is underdeveloped, you are better off in a less demanding field. The casualty rates are high among men who can't take it when the going is hard. In the long run, how well you do in a new assignment depends on your stamina.

One gloomy evening, not long before Appomattox, Robert E. Lee and the few survivors of his general staff were sitting around a small campfire trying to determine how they could get the remnants of the Army of Northern Virginia out of the encircling embrace of the vast Federal forces. The military situation was chaotic. General Lee had only fragmentary reports on which to base his plans, and he and his lieutenants hardly knew what troops were still available. While they were downheartedly discussing what to do, they heard the steady rhythm of the marching feet of an approaching infantry brigade.

Who were these soldiers? Lee did not expect any of his troops to be coming from the direction of the sounds. Was it a break-through? The moment was an ominous one. But Lee's relieved smile broke the tension.

The familiar route-step chant of a battle-worn Texas brigade identified the newcomers; the chant, a Texas paraphrase of a Biblical proverb.

> *The race is not to them what's got*
> *The longest legs to run,*
> *Nor the battle to those people*
> *What shoots the biggest gun.*

The Texans were moving up to take their place in the final battleline of what they already knew to be a lost cause. No one had expected them to arrive, for it had been assumed that they had long since been cut off and taken prisoner. But the men of the Texas brigade had fought through and were now moving into their last position of a lost war because it was their duty to be there. They had character and pride.

These two ingredients—character and pride—must be part of the make-up of the competitive executive. If you have these qualities and you also have the technical knowledge required to do your job, you will do all right in your new assignment. Problems like getting established in a new community, winning the acceptance of new associates, arranging for your children's schooling, and developing a pleasant social life are temporary. They will work out with time. The main thing is the job. Never allow side issues to sidetrack you and prevent you from giving your best effort to your assignment.

The resourceful executive knows that stamina is the backbone of all progress, even personal progress. If you are willing to accept reasonable risks and to keep plugging along to implement what you believe are sound and practical long-term decisions, you will probably be rewarded with responsibility that will not come even to some of your more talented but less competitive colleagues who always try to sidestep trouble, who give up and go home.

"Duty," said Robert E. Lee, "is the most sublime word in the English language." If you have accepted the responsibility of company leadership, your willingness to do your full duty at all times will determine your success on a new assignment—in your present company or somewhere else.